THE
YOUTH'S MEMORITER,
AND
ENGLISH EXERCISE BOOK,

IN TWO PARTS;

CONTAINING A RATIONAL

GRAMMAR OF THE ENGLISH LANGUAGE,

IN WHICH CASES, MOODS, COMPOUND TENSES, AND THE NUMBERS
AND PERSONS OF OUR VERBS HAVE BEEN REJECTED;

A VERBAL ANALYSIS,

OR A METHOD OF ACQUIRING THE SIGNIFICATIONS OF WORDS BY
A KNOWLEDGE OF THEIR COMPONENT
PARTS OR ELEMENTS;

AND

ORTHOGRAPHICAL EXERCISES,

UPON A PLAN ENTIRELY NEW,

COMPRISING IN ONE VOLUME ALL THAT IS NECESSARY FOR AN ENGLISH
SCHOLAR TO COMMIT TO MEMORY,
AND ALL THE EXERCISES USUALLY PUT INTO HIS HANDS.

Intended for the Use of Schools and private Tuition.

BY HENRY YOUNG.

LONDON:
WHITTAKER, TREACHER, AND CO. AVE-MARIA-LANE.

TO BE HAD OF ALL BOOKSELLERS.

1832.

SPALDING: PRINTED BY T. ALBIN.

INTRODUCTION.

IN compiling an elementary work, the primary consideration is simplicity; and in proportion as we depart from this fundamental principle, we create a corresponding confusion in the minds of those whom it is our intention to enlighten. That the greater part of our school books are eminently deficient in this respect must be evident to every liberal minded instructor. For it cannot be denied that the materials of education lie scattered over a vast extent of surface, and are not only disfigured by a superabundance of technicalities, but are for the most part enveloped in a cumbrous mass of extraneous matter. Our school grammars are loaded with useless and perplexing distinctions—our expositors, instead of leading the pupil through the fertile field of derivation, present an appalling catalogue of words with their dry meanings—and our orthographical exercise books, by their prolixity and incongruity, tend rather to bewilder the learner, than to impart " the just method of spelling words."

The chief design of this compilation is to remove some of the obstacles that lie at every avenue to a knowledge of the fundamental principles of our native language: and to simplify, as much as possible, and to bring within a narrower compass, three important branches of education, namely, ENGLISH GRAMMAR, ORTHOGRAPHY, and the SIGNIFICATIONS OF WORDS.

The book is divided into two parts. The first part contains a rational grammar of our language, syntactical exercises, and lessons for parsing. The second part comprises a verbal analysis, or tables of the component parts of words, foreign and Latin phrases in common use, arithmetical tables, and orthographical exercises. Combining in one volume all that is necessary for a merely English scholar to commit to memory, and all the exercises that are usually put into his hands.

In the following grammar the author has invariably conformed to the idiom of the language; he has rejected cases, moods, compound tenses, and the numbers and persons of our verbs, because he considers them to be mere imitations of Latin and Greek, introduced into our accidence without the indispensable ratification of reason and analogy.

If but a bare majority of those who have been taught by " the common method " were able to write their own language correctly, there would be some doubt as to the propriety of disturbing the present system. This is, however, by no means the case. In every town in England the greater part of the respectable inhabitants have committed Mr. Murray's rules to memory, and have, doubtless, gone through the whole of his exercises, yet nine out of ten are incapable of distinguishing one part of speech from another. We must therefore come to the conclusion, that the grammar of our native language is either too difficult to be attained without long and laborious study, or that the method of teaching it is radically bad. The English language, while it makes a near approach to the sublimity of the Greek and the majesty of the Latin, is, as regards its structure, proverbial for its simplicity. We are therefore naturally led to ask, How is it that a thing so simple should be difficult of attainment? The only answer that can be given to this rational enquiry is, that grammarians, by introducing " the artificial rules of other languages," have completely mystified our philological laws, and rendered this important branch of education an irksome and unprofitable study. Be it, then, our endeavour to point out wherein the difficulties lie, and, as far as we are able, to procure their removal.

The end of every distinctive appellation in grammar, is to show wherein a difference exists. Hence our nouns change their forms for the purpose of representing more objects than one —this is called *number*. The sexes of animals are shown by a change of the word—this we denominate *gender*. There are other variations, displaying correspondent distinctions, all of which are compendiously shewn by expressive terms. It is, however, clear to a demonstration, that, without a variation, we can adopt no distinctive word; for that which has not a being, cannot have a name. If therefore we introduce into grammar, terms for which we can find no distinction to warrant their adoption, we fall into the superlative absurdity of using names for things which never had an existence. Unless, then, it can be shewn that our words so modify their forms as to justify the introduction of cases, moods, and tenses, such appellations must be looked upon as gross barbarisms, which ought to be studiously avoided.

"Cases are usually defined to be certain terminations which nouns adopt to express the relations they bear to each other." Perhaps the following declension of a Latin noun may serve for illustration:

SINGULAR.   PLURAL.

CASES.	LATIN.	ENGLISH.	LATIN.	ENGLISH.
Nominative	Annus	A year	Anni	Years
Genitive	Anni	Of a year	Annorum	Of years
Dative & Ablative	Anno	To, with, &c. a year	Annis	To, with, &c. years
Accusative	Annum	A year	Annos	Years
Vocative	Anne	O year		

On comparing the translation in the above example with the original word, we immediately perceive an essential difference. The Latin noun *annus* yields to certain changes of termination, whilst its equivalent *year* is restricted to one unvarying form throughout, except indeed with regard to number: and in order to assign a perfect identity of meaning, we are reduced to the necessity of calling in the aid of other words. It is therefore evident that case cannot maintain the same import in both languages. For if, in one language, it be employed to exhibit the variations of single words only, how can it, in another language, have relation to a collection of words, none of which admit the slightest change? As Latin nouns vary their forms to adapt them to the circumstances of situation, it became necessary to devise a compendious method of pointing out their variations. Hence the utility of case in that language. But, as English nouns admit no changes of termination with regard to position, their arrangement in a sentence cannot be mistaken; case, therefore, with regard to them, must be entirely gratuitous.

The following is considered to be the declension of an English noun:

CASE.	SINGULAR.	PLURAL.
Nominative	A man	Men
Possessive	A man's	Men's
Objective	A man	Men

That form of our noun which is usually denominated the possessive case, is certainly a variation of the same word, and consequently creates a distinction. It will therefore be contended by some, that at all events, we have two cases. But if we drop the objective case, and retain the nominative and the possessive, a noun, when it represents the object of an action or of a relation, would be placed in the awkward dilemma of being in no case at all. A circumstance which would create a greater anomaly in the language, and cause more perplexity than the retention of the three cases. It is better then to renounce the idea of declension altogether, and assign to the possessive form of our noun a separate consideration, and give it a name that shall signify its peculiarities, and render its meaning intelligible. The possessive case, or, as the author has termed it, the genitive noun, is in fact nothing more than a noun converted into an adjective, and serves, as all adjectives do, to define the substantive with which it is joined. Thus we define a *girl's* school, or a *boy's* school, upon the same principle that we define a *large* school or a *small* school.

It will perhaps be contended that case is not merely identical with termination, but that its true nature is to represent nouns under different aspects or circumstances. If this definition be admitted, we shall have as many cases as there are aspects under which a noun may be viewed. By a *man*—with a *man*—for a *man*—she loves the *man*—the boy struck the *man*, would, upon this principle, be separate and independent cases, for it is evident that each combination of words represents man under totally different circumstances or aspects; we might, therefore, as we have no changes of termination to limit our conceptions, multiply cases without end. Case is indeed but another word for variation, and it is probable that had nouns in the learned languages been restricted to one form, we should never have thought of case at all. As the positions of our nouns, in a sentence, can be clearly pointed out by simply considering the substantive as the subject of the verb, or the object of an action, or of a relation, as it may occasionlly represent the one or the other, it is much better to rid the language of this " exotic term " than to perplex the learner by the retention of unnecessary technicalities.

We now offer a few remarks with regard to the cases of our pronouns. " The genuine pronoun is a word which always stands by itself," or which supplies the place of a noun. How then can we allege such words as *my, thy, his, her, our, your, their, all,* and *such,* to be pronouns, when it is evident that they are invariably used in connexion with a substantive? Their nature or property is to define nouns, or to distinguish them from others of the same kind; they are therefore adjectives and not pronouns. The same may be said of the possessive cases of our pronouns. *Mine* and *thine*, for instance, are merely the altered forms of *my* and *thy*, used when the substantive is understood; as, these books are *mine*, those are *thine*, that is, these books are *my* books, those are *thy* books. Indeed " *mine* and *thine* were formerly used *before* a substantive." At most, our pronouns are susceptible of but two cases, the nominative and the objective. The existence of these distinctive forms the author is ready to concede. But having rejected the cases of our nouns, he has, in order to prevent confusion, simply divided personal pronouns into nominative and objective without annexing the word case.

We next proceed to shew the propriety of rejecting the moods, compound tenses, and the numbers and persons of our verbs.

Mr. Murray defines mood to be " a particular *form* of the verb, shewing the manner in which the being, action, or passion, is represented." No one, it is presumed, will doubt the correctness of this definition, especially as it proceeds from authority. But how, it may be demanded, can mood belong to our language, wherein the impress of this particular form cannot be traced, as will be seen by the following example of what are alleged to be English moods?

MOOD.	VERB.	MOOD.	VERB.
Indicative	I *love*	Infinitive	To *love*
Potential	I may *love*	Imperative	*Love* thou
Subjunctive	If I *love*		

We here discern no variation of the word to constitute Mr. Murray's particular *form*, consequently, either his definition must be a mere illusion, or there can be no such thing as mood in the English language. He, however, contends " that the conjugation or *variation* of verbs in the English language, is effected almost *entirely* by the means of *auxiliaries*," and further adds, " we must accommodate ourselves to this circumstance, and do that by their assistance, which has been done in the learned languages in another manner, namely, by *varying* the *form* of the verb itself. " If we are to allow such an invasion of our understandings, as to admit that an assemblage of words constitutes a particular form of one word, there is no saying to what lengths we may not go, or by what standard we are to determine between truth and fiction. Upon this principle we are justified in considering—*to a man*, the dative case—*by a man*, the ablative case—and *through a man*, a case which has not yet approached the grammatic font.

Mood is farther defined " to signify various intentions of the mind, and various modifications and circumstances of action." This indeed is applicable to every sentence in the language. *I rode on horseback yesterday*, is one circumstance of action—*I rode in a chaise yesterday* is another circumstance of action—*I will ride now,—I will ride to-morrow*, are different intentions of the mind. Every sentence must contain a finite verb, representing an action or a state, attended by circumstances, or intentions of the mind, and must be necessarily modified by words with which it is associated. So that upon this principle, every sentence will be a different mood, consequently, we must have as many moods in our language as there are sentences. At all events, we must have as many moods as auxiliaries, for it is evident that each auxiliary has a signification of its own. *I ride—I may ride —I can ride—I will ride—I shall ride—let him ride —he must ride*—express different modifications of action, they have, therefore, each an equitable claim to be accounted an independent mood. It appears, then, after all, that mood is restricted to languages wherein verbs undergo certain alterations, in order to agree with certain circumstances of action, or certain intentions of the mind; therefore, as English verbs disclaim all such alterations of form, they cannot be entitled to the distinction of mood.

The following partial conjugation of the Latin verb *Amo, I love,* compared with its translation, will tend, in some measure, to rectify our notions with regard to mood:

MOODS.	LATIN.	ENGLISH.
Indicative	Am*o*	I *love*
Potential	Am*em*	I may or can *love*
Imperative	Am*a*	*Love* thou
Infinitive	Am*are*	To *love*

Compound tenses, like our moods, are founded upon the principle of combining words with one another under the rules of etymology, and are therefore fit objects for expulsion. Indeed it is doubtful whether tense be within the pale of our language at all. That form of a regular verb which the author has denominated the past tense, is nothing more than a perfect participle. As, however, the caprice of custom has created several past forms to our irregular verbs, it was thought more eligible to retain this distinction than to stand upon too great a nicety. At all events, our verbs can claim but two legitimate tenses, the present and the past, as will be evident upon inspection of the following example:

Present tense	I *love*
Imperfect tense	I *loved*
Perfect tense	I have *loved*
Pluperfect tense	I had *loved*
First future tense	I shall *love*
Second future tense	I shall have *loved*

Here then we have but two distinct forms of the

verb—*love*, and *loved*. The simple form, if we allow the existence of time in our verbs at all, is rightly enough denominated the present tense; but upon what principle we are to represent an *imperfect* action by means of the *perfect* participle is certainly very mysterious. For when an action or event is passed and finished, it has reached a point of perfection beyond which it cannot go. This tense then ought to be called the perfect rather than the imperfect. The fact is, the time of an action or event is not determined by the verb itself, but, as Mr. Lennie justly observes, " by the drift or scope of the sentence. " *I will ride on horseback*, by no means points to future time, it merely expresses an intention of the mind, without any regard to time whatever ; and yet *I will ride*, is said to be *a verb* of the future tense. It is true the variations of verbs in the learned languages are not sufficient of themselves to determine the precise period of an action or event; they merely, by uniting with the root of the word, coincide with the time pointed out by other words.

Greek and Latin tenses are however built upon the substantial ground of inflexion, and as far as inflexion goes, we are compelled to admit a distinction. But Mr. Murray says, " it is indisputable that the principal verb, or rather its participle and an auxiliary, constitute a regular tense in the Latin and Greek, " and from this he infers, that " we may apply it to English verbs." The truth is, Greek and Latin verbs are by no means uniform with regard to the number of their tenses. Passive verbs in the Latin, for instance, have but three tenses in the indicative mood instead of five, the usual number, and but two in the potential mood. To supply this deficiency, the Romans were compelled to use, in a sentence, a participle and an auxiliary. These combinations, it is admitted, are *called* regular tenses; but when we consider that they form a total departure from the analogy of Latin conjugation, it is more rational to look upon them as mere deficiencies, than to carry the idea of moods and tenses farther than we are warranted by inflexion.

It is certainly very capricious to limit our cases to three, and at the same time to adopt all the moods and tenses of the Latin. Why not at once force upon us *all* the cases too? And why should we shrink from the adoption of a dual number, since it exists in the *Greek?* For it would be less ridiculous to consider *arms, hands, eyes,* and *feet,* the dual number, than to assume that *I might have been loved,* is a tense of the verb. If it be so desirable to cast our language in classic mould, why not rescind our grammatic laws altogether, and in imitation of Latin and Greek, cement our prepositions, articles, and nouns, to form cases, and our pronouns, auxiliaries, and principal verbs, to form moods, tenses, numbers, and persons? Perhaps the following model may tend to further this *desideratum:*

NOUNS.	VERBS.
Manthe	Lovedmighthavei
Mantheof	Lovedmightsthavethou
Mantheto	Lovedmighthavehe
Manthe	Lovedmighthavewe
Mano!	Lovedmighthaveyou
Manthein	Lovedmighthavethey

This would be assimilation with a vengeance, yet it is sound doctrine.

It is doubtless considered by some, that the right construction of sentences in our language mainly depends on the retention of moods and tenses. Is it then likely that an Englishman can mistake the applications of our auxiliaries? That he would use *shall* instead of *can,* or *will* instead of *may?* We cannot for a moment suppose that a native of Britain would join *have* or *am* to the simple form of the verb, for there needs no ghost to inform us that such phraseologies as the following are improper: *I am sit, I have walk.* And with regard to the grouping of our verbs and participles, so as to coincide with the times of their actions or events, the only difficulty lies in ascertaining when to adopt or reject *have* and its past tense *had.* But the adjustment of these words must be determined by the laws of syntax, not by the rules of etymology; nor is it at all necessary that they should be roted in a conjugate form. The conjugation of an English verb necessarily occasions the greatest confusion in the mind of a learner; for when he is running over a rhodomontade of moods and tenses, he naturally expects that the auxiliaries and principal verbs should at all times be in close connexion with each other; however, on his arrival at syntax, he finds that not only words may intervene between them, but that they may be also separated by phrases. Thus the mystic chain is at length broken, and the learner compelled at last to treat our auxiliaries as independent words. As, however, by far the greater part of our youths have not sufficient time to waste in arriving at this *ultimatum*, we are highly culpable if, instead of conducting them through the perplexing mazes of cases, moods, and tenses, we neglect to place them at once on the high road of truth.

Grammar does not enforce laws upon a language; it merely collects together the phraseological usages of a country, and presents them in a digested form, in order that they may be more readily understood. Therefore, whenever we, either for the sake of uniformity, or for the purpose of assimilation, impose upon a language that which cannot be supported by reason and analogy, we deviate from the line of rectitude, and ascribe to grammar a dictatorial power to which it has no claim. The grammarian ought to treat the language as he finds it, not to engraft upon it the uncongenial branches of other languages. Truth ought to be his guide, and he ought above all things to avoid visionary theories, " artificial contrivances," and "subtle kinds of reasoning." Hence, then, as the combining of words under the rules of etymology is ratified neither by reason nor analogy, there can be no such thing as moods and compound tenses in our language.

The following example of a farther conjugation of the Latin verb *amo*, will serve to shew the true nature of tense:

TENSES.	LATIN.	ENGLISH.
Present	Amo	I *love*
Imperfect	Am*abam*	I *loved*
Perfect	Am*avi*	I have *loved*
Pluperfect	Am*averam*	I had *loved*
Future	Am*abo*	I shall *love*

With regard to the numbers and persons of our verbs, we may be said to possess the shadow of inflexion, and but the shadow. In our language, we find but two personal terminations; *s*, which is annexed to the verb in the present tense only, and *st*, which is admitted in both tenses. The pronoun *thou* is the only word that occasions the adoption of *st*; and the termination *s* is never employed but when the verb has *he*, *she*, *it*, or a substantive of the singular number for its subject, as will be seen by the following example:

SINGULAR.

PERSON.	PRESENT TIME.	PAST TIME.
1	I love	I loved
2	Thou love*st*	Thou loved*st*
3	He, &c. loves	He, &c. loved

PLURAL.

1	We love	We loved
2	You love	You loved
3	They love	They loved

Mr. Murray and others give it as a rule that "a verb must agree with its nominative case in number and person." When this rule is put into the hands of a learner, he naturally looks for a variation of the verb adapted to the three persons in each number. This, however, proves to be a miserable deception, for instead of six variations he finds but two, a circumstance which adds greatly to his perplexity. If our verbs agree with their nominative cases in number, how is it that the first person singular bears the same form as the three persons of the plural number; and if we are to admit the distinction of person, why do the three persons of the plural number end alike? Instead, then, of perplexing the pupil by conjuring up the mere phantoms of a dead language, it is much more rational to point out, in a direct manner, when these terminations ought to be adopted, and to show under what circumstances they ought to be rejected.

The following example of some of the personal terminations of a Latin verb, contrasted with ours, may, perhaps, place the subject in a clearer point of view:

SINGULAR.

PERSON.	LATIN.	ENGLISH.
1	Amo	I love
2	Amas	Thou lovest
3	Amat	He, &c. loves

PLURAL.

1	Amamus	We love
2	Amatis	You love
3	Amant	They love

If an individual, in order to assimilate the learned languages to his own, were to transform the inflexions of those languages into separate or independent words, he would richly deserve, for his temerity, all the classic abuse that would doubtless be heaped upon him. Yet strange as it may appear, we can, in this enlightened age, submit to "the warping" of our own language to meet the idioms of Latin and Greek. Englishmen, where is your patriotism, to suffer such inroads upon your noble language? And instead of maintaining its independence, to allow the concealment of its beauties under classic " shreds and patches!" The free-born sons of Albion, then, after all their boasting, are the oddest slaves in the world, for they have submitted their minds and *tongues* to the thraldom of two *dead* languages.

To impose declensions and conjugations upon our language, under the childish pretext of their existence in the Latin, is no less absurd than to consider the monarchy of Britain a triumvirate, merely because that form of government once existed among the Romans. When we can revoke the Divine decree passed at the building of Babel's impious tower, then, but not till then, will we conform our language to the idiom of the Latin—then, but not till then, will we barter simplicity for prolixity—the natural order of our ideas for the inverted phraseology of the ancient tongues.

It will doubtless be contended that these appendages to grammar facilitate the acquirement of Latin and Greek, and on that account they ought to be retained. But is it reasonable that we should subvert the order, and desert the simplicity of our vernacular tongue, to suit the convenience of those who are to acquire what is termed a classical education? Certainly not. Let such as delight in poring over the volumes of antiquity grope their way as well as they can. But let every language rest upon its own merits, and be learnt by its own peculiarities. This, by affording the pupil who studies them an opportunity of comparing their idioms, will secure to him a correct knowledge of the structure of each, without reducing him to the necessity of a fruitless attempt at assimilation.

Many think that without a knowledge of Latin, it is impossible to have a clear conception of English grammar. The prevalence of this absurd idea, has for ages acted like a magic spell, and chained down many a bright genius who would otherwise have shone resplendent in the hemisphere of British literature.

But happily for our national credit, several popular writers of the present day, nobly disdaining these bonds, have shown by their compositions that our language possesses ample means for maintaining its own rights, and discribing its own structure. Would it not be accounted almost a crime to disparage the inimitable productions of the bard of Avon? And yet he, it seems, was no classic. Shakespear, like a mighty magician, not only broke this classic spell, and set the sticklers for Latin and Greek at defiance, but created a thousand charms by which he unfolded the capabilities of his native language.

It is not here attempted to deny that classical scholars have written in their own language with purity and elegance, but we are not to infer from this that they depended upon an acquaintance with the learned tongues as a medium for understanding their own. It therefore behoves every parent to see that his children, before they enter upon the study of other languages, are well versed in English.

If the reader will but take the trouble to look around his own neighbourhood, and among his own acquaintances, he will find that scarcely one in ten of those who have been educated at a grammar-school, can either write the English language correctly, or translate a single passage of Latin or Greek. To what are we to attribute this circumstance—but to the foolish attempt to reconcile antipathies? Thus by aiming at that which is impossible—the consolidation of the different structures of languages—the pupil goes into the world half educated, and must continue so, unless, when his judgment is matured, he is led to view things as they are, and has time and inclination to root out the errors implanted in his mind by this barbarous method.

The author is by no means desirous to under-rate the learned languages; on the contrary, he believes that to those who *thoroughly understand them*, they are a constant source of mental pleasure. All that he contends for is the paramount importance of our own, and the necessity for throwing off its classic guise, in order that it may appear in its native character. Nor is he vain enough to imagine that he has, in every instance, succeeded in his attempt at simplification. However, the barbarisms pointed out in the foregoing remarks have been avoided, and, he trusts, the language placed upon its own basis. The circumstance that the subject might have been in abler hands, will not invalidate the principles laid down in the following work, and fortified as those principles are, not by any ability on the part of the author, but by reason—by analogy—by utility—and by truth—it will require all the artillery of Greek and Latin, and all the thunder of the gods and goddesses of classic Greece and Rome, to overturn them. There is much more merit, as far as talent goes, in adroitly forcing down our throats the useless lumber of cases, moods, and tenses, than in pursuing the plain and obvious course which the author has followed. He, therefore, claims but little credit for what he has done. The road is direct enough, if we will but walk in it, and barring a few false steps " which flesh is heir to," we need not trip in travelling. But had our grammarians taken this plain and open path, they could not have shewn their dexterity in climbing over hills and mountains, when they might have pursued their journey at an easier rate. The author, no doubt, has preconceived notions, and established principles, however false, to contend against. These he disregards, being well persuaded that the intellectual light which illuminates our country, has exposed the absurdity of submitting to the *dictum* of the classic few, who have arrogated to themselves the exclusive right to dispense the laws of literature.

The design of the Verbal Analysis is to teach the significations of words, by giving the meanings of their component parts. This plan will secure to a learner the knowledge of a greater number of words, and in less time than by the usual method. When the component parts or elements are known, they may be recognised in every situation; and as they always retain their original significations, and contribute those significations towards forming the meanings of words of which they constitute a part, it is evident that he who has a complete store of them, will hardly ever require the aid of a dictionary. In almost every expositor, we find from six to eight thousand words, some of them of seven or eight syllables, with their dry explanations. The Analysis contains less than fifteen hundred elements, by the combinations of which from ten to twelve thousand words are formed, without taking into account those of obvious meaning. Out of this number we may fairly reckon from three to four thousand not found in any school book.

Words least likely to be known by the common course of things, are such as are derived from Latin and Greek, and to the elements from those languages, the author has, with a few exceptions, confined himself.

The orthographical exercises consist of single words, with a clue to their correct spelling. In every composition, the same words are continually recurring, so that a learner has to wade through a considerable number of such as are already known, before he can arrive at those to which he is a stranger. This occasions a loss of time. Besides, words when associated do not make a sufficient impression upon the mind to insure their permanent retention.

In compiling the following sheets, the author has availed himself of most of our standard works upon grammar and derivation, from which many of the examples and exercises have been extracted, and a considerable portion of the ideas have been adopted.

Doubtless, the following work will be looked upon as a bold experiment, and will, perhaps, be treated by some as a daring innovation. But when it was considered that our numerous school grammars were but servile copies of each other—that every succeeding expositor was but a slight variation from its predecessor—and that the generality of our orthographical exercise books were but varied hues of the same colour, there was, independently of the reasons already assigned, an inducement to desert " the beaten track." Originality, however, in the present day, is scarcely attainable. The author, aware that others had *partially* laid open the direct road to English grammar, imagined, that in *totally* rejecting foreign rules and useless terms, he was venturing upon an untrodden path. In this he was mistaken. The subject of rational grammar had previously been well discussed in an able article in the " London Encyclopœdia," a circumstance with which he was wholly unacquainted until he had placed the greater part of his manuscript in the hands of the printer. The discovery, however, inspired him with renewed confidence, for in attempting the entire subversion of an established system, it is no trifling satisfaction to have an authority of such unequivocal talent as Mr. Gilchrist, the writer of the article in question.

A number of youths have, for the last six months, been studying English grammar from the author's manuscript; and have, notwithstanding the disadvantages of merely oral instruction, made greater proficiency than some of them had previously done in roting Mr. Murray's rules for several years before; thus satisfactorily proving, by the unerring test of experiment, the rationality and utility of the following simplification.

In the anxious pursuit of his subject, and in aiming at the utmost simplicity of style, and brevity of expression, the author has been unconsciously led into errors, some of which he has discovered and pointed out in the " errata." The rest will, no doubt, be readily seen by others. Though he deeply regrets the occurrence of those errors, he hopes they are not, in any case, sufficient to obscure his meaning, or materially to detract from what little merit the work may possess.

A slight investigation of the subject under consideration, is sufficient to convince every unprejudiced reader, that the only legitimate " system of education" consists in simply written elementary works. With these the teacher would be enabled to conduct the business of his school at a considerable reduction of labour and perplexity on his part, and the certainty of rapid and permanent improvement on the part of his pupils. How far the author has succeeded in producing a book that, as regards the subjects of which it treats, will tend to these desirable results, must be left to the decision of his enlightened countrymen.

Spalding, Lincolnshire, 1832.

DIRECTIONS FOR USING THE BOOK.

The rules of the grammar should be committed to memory, not in a superficial manner, but so as to be repeated without hesitation. In order to accomplish this, the pupil should go over them until he is perfect. A great deal has been lost through inattention to this particular. The mind, in its unexpanded state, cannot fully comprehend the nature of things; but if rules be indelibly imprinted on the memory, the learner will have in store a valuable quantity of raw materials for time and a matured judgment to digest.

In committing the tables of the Analysis to memory the element, when dashes fall under it, should be repeated first, and the meanings afterwards. Thus, for instance, the prefix *para*, at page 77, must be repeated in the following manner—*para*—*through, with, contrary to, by the side of.* When dashes fall under the meanings, the whole of the elements must be repeated first—for example, the prefixes *sym, syn, syl, sys*, at the same page, must be repeated thus—*sym, syn, syl, sys, with, together.*

Annu,	a circle
——	a year
Enni	——

and elements similarly circumstanced, must be repeated as follow—*annu, a circle, a year*—*enni, a year.*

It is not necessary that the examples should be committed to memory.

DIRECTIONS FOR USING THE BOOK.   XXIII

The method of analysing the words at page 167, will be seen by the following example:

ACRIMONY.

Acri	sharp
mony	substantive, termination of the thing.
Acrimony	sharpness.

CHRONOLOGY.

Chron	time
log	a discourse or word
y	substantive of the thing
Chronology	a discourse, or a word upon time.

REDUNDANT.

Re	again
d	added
und	a wave
Redundant	a waving again, i. e. overflowing.

TRANSPIRE.

Trans	beyond
spir	(s is dropt) to breathe
e	added
Transpire	to breathe beyond, i. e. to escape.

There are some terminations that are either so limited in their applications, or that have not the effect of changing words from one part of speech to another, as not to entitle them to a place in the analysis. The *e* in transpire is an instance.

ERRATA.

Page 7 line 6, for *hers* read *her*.
— 8 —— 11, after *I*, insert *we*.
— —— —— 12, after *it*, insert *they and them*.
— 10 —— 3, for *point out* read *agree with*.
— 17 —— 22, for *shown* read *shewn*, or for *shew* and *shewed* read *show* and *showed*.
— 40 —— 12, after *two*, insert *or more*.
— —— —— 14, after *both*, insert *or all*.
— 70 —— 16,⎫ the preposition is misplaced,
— —— —— 26,⎬ in direct opposition to one of
— 71 —— 4,⎭ the rules.
— 96 —— 21, for *catastrophy*, read *catastrophe*.
— 121 —— 6, for *ply*, read *pli*
— 201 —— 13, under the head of Orthography, after *w* and *y*, insert *except*. The author regrets that the omission of this word completely reverses the meaning of the sentence.

In the table of the first class of irregular verbs, page 14, the capitals, from an oversight, have been omitted to the greater part of the words, which gives them the appearance of being mere variations of the first column, whereas they are independent words.

In the numeration table, page 157, after hundreds of millions, for *billions*, read *thousands of millions*, to the end of the table.

The 167th page of the work is immediately succeeded by page 198, causing an apparent hiatus of 31 pages.

THE YOUTH'S MEMORITER.

PART THE FIRST.

ENGLISH GRAMMAR.

ENGLISH GRAMMAR is the art of speaking and writing the English language according to established usage.

It is commonly divided into four parts: ORTHOGRAPHY*, ETYMOLOGY, SYNTAX, and PROSODY.

ETYMOLOGY.

ETYMOLOGY treats of the nature of words, explains their modifications, and traces their derivations†.

Words are divided into classes, called parts of speech.

There are nine PARTS OF SPEECH: the ARTICLE, the SUBSTANTIVE, the ADJECTIVE, the PRONOUN, the VERB,

---

* Orthography is made a distinct subject in another part of this work, it is therefore merely named here.

† The verbal analysis in the second part.

the ADVERB, the PREPOSITION, the CONJUNCTION, and the INTERJECTION.

DIRECTIONS FOR DISTINGUISHING THE PRINCIPAL PARTS OF SPEECH.

A word that can be properly joined to *I am thinking of*, or *I am thinking of a, an,* or *the,* is a Substantive: as,

> I am thinking of *GOD.* I am thinking of a *book.* I am thinking of the *sky.* I am thinking of *virtue.* I am thinking of *nothing.* I am thinking of *something.*

Every word that will take *thing* or *things,* or any other substantive after it, is an Adjective, except a, an, and the: as,

> *Good* thing, *bad* thing, *wise* men, *many* things, *one* book.

A word that will take *I, thou, he,* or *we* before it, is a Verb; and if it will take *him, her,* or *them* after it, it is a Transitive Verb: as,

> I *love,* thou *walkest,* we *sit,* I *love* her, she *struck* him.

Words that answer to the questions *how? how much? when?* or *where?* joined to a verb or an adjective, are Adverbs: as,

> An exceedingly great man. How great? *exceedingly.* She loves him sincerely. How does she love him? *sincerely.*

A word that will take *him, her,* or *them* after it,

but which will not take *I, thou, he* or *we* before it, is a Preposition: as,

With him, *for* her, *to* them.

A word that is used to connect words and sentences is a Conjunction: as,

He *and* she. The man *or* the woman. They came with her, *but* they went away without her.

ARTICLES.

There are but three Articles; *a, an,* and *the.*

SUBSTANTIVES.

Substantives, or Nouns, are the names of persons, places, or things: as,

Boy, girl, school, virtue, goodness, blackness, Thomas, London.

Names given to persons, places, or things, to distinguish them from others of the same kind, are Proper Substantives; all other substantives are common: as,

Common. *Boy, city, river, ship,*
Proper. *Thomas, London, Thames, the Ocean,*
Com. *horse, coach, man.*
Prop. *Eclipse, the Highflyer, William Smith.*

Gender.*

Substantives have two *genders*; the *masculine*, which denotes the male sex, and the *feminine*, which denotes the female sex.

* Directions for converting masculine nouns into feminine are given in the exercises.

Substantives which have no distinction of sex are called *neuter*: as,

Masculine. *Man, boy, bull, horse.*
Feminine. *Woman, girl, cow, mare.*
Neuter. *Book, school, town, house.*

Our language admits of a few deviations from these rules. The *sun* is masculine. The *moon*, as well as *ships*, &c. is feminine.

Some words include both the genders: as,

Parent, child, cousin, friend.

Number *.

A substantive is of the *singular* number when it represents but one person or thing, and of the *plural* number when it represents more than one: as,

Singular. *Man, woman, boy, town, book.*
Plural. *Men, women, boys, towns, books.*

Some substantives have no singular and others no plural form: as,

No singular. *Ashes, riches, bellows, scissors, &c.*
No plural. *Wheat, pitch, gold, silver, &c.*

The Genitive Noun.

The Genitive Noun is formed by adding *s* to the substantive, with a comma (') called the *apostrophe*: as,

My *father's* house. The *boy's* book.

If the plural substantive end in *s,* or the singular in

---

* **Rules** for the formation of the plural number of nouns will be found in the exercises.

ss, the genitive *s* is omitted, but the apostrophic comma is retained: as,

>Singular. *For righteousness' sake.*
>Plural. *On eagles' wings.*

Person.

The *first* person is the person speaking, the *second* the person spoken to, and the *third* the person or thing spoken of; hence all substantives are of the *third* person, because they are always spoken of.

ADJECTIVES.

Adjectives are of three sorts. 1. Such as express the qualities, quantities, and sizes of substantives. 2. Such as point out their number. 3. Such as define them: as,

> Quality. A *good* boy. A *bad* man. A *virtuous* girl.
> Size and Quantity. *Tall* trees. A *large* house. *Much* money.
> Number. *One* book. *Two* houses. The *first* tree.
> Definitive. *This* man. *Some* houses. *Several* trees.

Comparison.

Most adjectives denoting quality and size have two degrees of comparison; the *comparative* and the *superlative*. The comparative degree either raises or lowers one of two persons or things above or below the other: the superlative raises or lowers one out of many above or below the rest. The comparative is formed by adding *r* or *er* to the simple form of the adjective, and the superlative by adding *st* or *est*: as,

Simple form. *Wide, long, short, wise.*
Comparative. *Wider, longer, shorter, wiser.*
Superlative. *Widest, longest, shortest, wisest.*

Many adjectives of quality do not admit of comparison: as,

Golden, right, universal.

The following are irregularly formed:

SIMP.	COMP.	SUP.
Good	*better*	*best.*
Bad	*worse*	*worst.*
Little	*less*	*least.*
Much or *many*	*more*	*most.*
Near	*nearer*	*nearest* or *next.*
Old	*older*	*oldest* or *eldest.*
Late	*later*	*latest* or *last.*

More or *most* joined to an adjective in its simple form points out the degree of comparison: as,

Wise, more wise, most wise.

Ish, rather, and *too,* denote a slight excess of quality: as,

Salt*ish*, *rather* salt, *too* salt.

There is a certain form of the verb, called the participle, frequently used as an adjective: as,

A *learned* man, from the verb *to learn.*
A *loving* child, from the verb *to love.*

Adjectives of number undergo no change; they are either cardinal or ordinal: as,

Cardinal. *One, five, ten, hundred, thousand.*
Ordinal. *First, fifth, tenth, hundredth, thousandth.*

Adjectives of number are frequently used as substantives: as,

Take care of the little *ones*. For *ten's* sake.

The principal definitive adjectives are, *this, these, that, those, every, any, another, others, all, such, both, few, several, divers, sundry, my, thy, his, hers, its, our, your, their, mine, thine, hers, ours, yours, theirs,* and *whose, which, what,* and *that,* which are also used as relative pronouns.

My, mine, our, and ours, are of the *first* person; thy, thine, your, and yours, are of the *second* person; and his, her, hers, their, and theirs, are of the *third* person.

Substantives added to other substantives assume the nature of adjectives: as,

A *mahogany* table, a *tea* kettle.

The genitive noun may be considered an adjective: as,

The *boy's* book. The *girl's* book.

" An adjective put without a substantive, with the article *the* before it, becomes a substantive in sense and meaning ": as,

The *good*. The *bad*. The *great*.

PRONOUNS.

A Pronoun is a word that is used instead of a substantive, or noun, to prevent the too frequent repetition of the same word.

Pronouns are either *personal* or *relative*.

Personal pronouns are divided into *nominative* and *objécitve*.

The nominative pronouns are *I*, *thou*, *he*, and *she*, which are of the singular number; and *we*, *ye*, and *they*, which are of the plural.

The objective pronouns are *me*, *him*, *her*, and *thee*, of the singular number; and *us* and *them*, of the plural.

You and *it* are both nominative and objective: *you* is of both numbers; *it* is singular.

He and *him* are masculine; *she* and *her* are feminine; and *it* is neuter.

I and *me* are of the first person; *thou*, *you*, *ye*, and *thee*, are of the second person; and *he*, *she*, *it*, are of the third person.

The relative pronouns are *who*, *whom*, and the definitive adjectives *whose*, *which*, *what*, and *that*.

Relatives stand for personal pronouns as well as for substantives, the words for which they stand being called their antecedents: as,

>She *who* called this morning. The man *that* lives at the corner.

Whose, *which*, *what*, and *that*, are definitive adjectives when they are joined to substantives, but in every other situation they are relative pronouns: as,

>Def. Adj. *Whose* book? *Which* boy? *What* day did you say? *That* man.
>
>Rel. Pron. The man *that* I sent. The tree *which* stands at the end of the walk.

Who, *whose*, and *whom*, are applied to persons; *which* to animals and things without life; *that* is applied to both persons and things; *what* is mostly equivalent to *that which*: as,

> The man *who* came this morning is the same *whom* you saw yesterday. The trees *which* I planted. This is *what* I wanted; i. e. *that which* I wanted.

VERB.

A Verb is a word which expresses the action, state, or condition of a person or thing: as,

> I *love*. He *walks*. The pen *is* bad.

Verbs are either *transitive* or *intransitive*.

Transitive verbs are such as will take substantives or objective pronouns after them: as,

> I *love her*. Charles *struck James*. The dog *bit* the *man*.

Intransitive verbs are those which cannot take substantives or objective pronouns after them, without prepositions: as,

> I *walk*. I *walk* with him. I *sit*. I *sit* on a chair.

Transitive verbs denote actions that pass from an agent or subject to an object; intransitive verbs are those which confine the action or event to the agent: as,

	AGENT or SUBJECT.	VERB.	OBJECT.
Trans.	John	*loves*	Mary.
Intrans.	Mary	*walks*.	

Verbs are either *principal* or *auxiliary*.

Principal verbs denote the *actions*, *states*, or *conditions* of persons or things: as,

> *Love, learn, deplore, involve, run, walk.*

Auxiliary verbs are mostly used in a sentence with principal verbs, either to modify their *meaning*, or to point out the *time* of their actions or events; they are,

Shall, will, may, can, am, be, do, have, let, must, and *ought*.

Am, have, be, and do, are *principal* verbs when they are not followed by other verbs: as,

I *am* here. Let it *be* mine. I *have* it. I *do* nothing.

Verbs, whether principal or auxiliary, are *finite* when they stand alone, or when they are placed first in a series or set of verbs: as,

I *love*. Thou *walkest*. I *do* run. I *did* read.

I *might* have been robbed.

Perfect participles, when used as past tenses, are also *finite* verbs: as,

I *walked* with him. I *heard* him talk. He *loved* me.

Verbs are *infinite*, that is, they have no relation to time, when set after verbs and participles to which they belong, or when they are joined to the preposition *to*: as,

I do *love*. I did *love*. I shall *walk*. I bid him do it. Seeing him *run*, &c. To *love*. To *play*.

Participles.

The Participle is a variation of the verb, forming a word which partakes also of the nature of an adjective: as,

Part. He is *running*. He has *learned* his lesson.
Adj. A *running* stream. A *learned* man.

There are two participles, the *perfect* and the *imperfect*.

The perfect participle is formed by adding *d* or *ed* to the verb, and the imperfect by adding *ing*: as,

 Verb. Love, learn, deplore, involve.
 Perf. Part. *Loved, learned, deplored, involved.*
 Imp. Part. *Loving, learning, deploring, involving.*

When participles are used as verbs, the imperfect represents the action as *going on* at the time referred to, but the perfect shews it to be *complete* and *finished* up to the period mentioned: as,

 Imp. I am *walking.* I was *learning.*
 Perf. I have *walked.* I had *learned.*

Tense or *time.*

The time when an action or event takes place is not pointed out by the verb, but by other words in the sentence: as,

 I shall go *to-morrow.* I saw him *yesterday.*

The verb, in its simple form, when it is not infinitive, agrees with present time, and forms what is called the present tense: as,

 I *see* him *now.* I *have this moment* left him.

The perfect participle, when used alone, constitutes the past tense and agrees with past time; but when it is joined in a sentence to *am, have,* and *be,* in any of their variations, it has no relation to time, being then employed merely to shew that the action or event is complete and finished: as,

 I *walked* home *last evening.* I *had walked* a mile *before* he overtook me.

The English language has no future tense. The time of a future action or event must be denoted by words or phrases pointing out the particular period referred to: I *will go*, merely expresses my present determination; I *will go to-morrow*, denotes a future action. Such combinations as, *I shall have been, I will have been*, &c. are used only when future time is denoted; they do not, however, establish a future tense, the time referred to being understood.

Imperfect participles never agree with time: as,

    I am *walking*. I was *walking*. I have been *walking*.

Present time, in grammar, is any period, part of which is considered to be in existence: as,

    This *minute, hour, day, week, month, year, century.*

The past is a period wherein we break the chain of connexion with the present, and limit the event to a time gone by: as,

    A *minute* or an *hour ago, yesterday,* last *week, month, year, century.*

Future time is any period to come: as,

    Next *minute, hour, day, month, year, century, to-morrow.*

Time may be indefinitely stated; it may be also understood: as,

    I *shall* go *some* day or *other*. I *mentioned* it *when* I called upon him. I *have* been loved.

A past time may be anterior to another past time: as,

    He *called* before I *went* out. The *week* before *last*.

One future time may be considered as prior to another future time: as,

I *shall* have dined *before* two o'clock.

Personal Terminations.*

The Personal Terminations are *s* or *es*; and *st* or *est*.

S or *es* is added to a verb in the present tense only: *st* or *est* is used in either tense.

In the Scriptures, and sometimes in solemn discourse, *th* or *eth* is added to the verb instead of *s* or *es*. *Will* and *shall* change their final *l* into *t* instead of taking *st* or *est*.

The following table of the auxiliaries exhibits all their variations.

Present.	Past.	Imp. Part.
Shall, shalt	should, shouldst	———
Will, wilt	would, wouldst	———
May, mayst	might, mightst	———
Can, canst	could, couldst	———
Am and be, art, is, are	was, wast, were	being.
Do, dost	did, didst	doing.
Have, hast, has or hath	had, hadst	having.
Let	———	———
Must	———	———
Ought	———	———

Done is the perfect participle of *do*, but is never

* This subject properly belongs to Syntax, where it is fully exemplified.

put for the past tense. *Be* is used as the infinitive of *am*, and *been* for its perfect participle.

Am, when used in a sentence with plural substantives and pronouns, is changed into *are* in the present tense and to *were* in the past.

The principal and regular verb *to love*, in its finite state, with every change that it can possibly undergo, is here given as a pattern of the rest.

Present.	Past & perf. part.	Imp. part.
Love	loved	loving.
Lovest	lovedst	
Loves or loveth		

Irregular Verbs.

Irregular Verbs are such as do not form their past tenses or perfect participles by the addition of *d* or *ed*; in every other respect they are managed the same as regular verbs.

A LIST OF THE PRINCIPAL IRREGULAR VERBS.

Those marked with an R *are also regular.*

1. Such as undergo no variation with regard to time, but have the present tense used for the past, or perfect participle.

Burst	cut	put	shed	slit, R.
Bid	hit	read	shread	split
Cast	hurt	rid	spit	spread
Cost	knit, R.	set	shut	thrust.

Bid has also *bade* for the past tense and *bidden* for its perfect participle. *Spit* is regular when it relates to meat for roasting.

ETYMOLOGY.

2. Such as have a past tense, or perfect participle, expressed by one word, but which is irregularly formed:

Present.	Past.	Present.	Past.
Abide	abode.	Pay	paid.
Bend	bent.	Rend	rent.
Bereave	bereft, R.	Ring	rung.
Beseech	besought.	Say	said.
Bind	bound.	Seek	sought.
Bite	bit.	Sell	sold.
Bleed	bled.	Send	sent.
Breed	bred.	Shine	shone, R.
Bring	brought.	Shoe	shod.
Build	built.	Shoot	shot.
Buy	bought.	Shrink	shrunk.
Catch	caught, R.	Sing	sung.
Cleave	cleft.	Sit	sat.
Cling	clung.	Sink	sunk.
Creep	crept.	Sleep	slept.
Deal	dealt, R.	Sling	slung.
Dig	dug, R.	Slink	slunk.
Dwell	dwelt, R.	Speed	sped.
Feed	fed.	Spring	sprung.
Feel	felt.	Spend	spent.
Fling	flung.	Spill	spilt, R.
Get	got.	Spin	spun.
Gild	gilt, R.	Stand	stood.
Gird	girt, R.	Stick	stuck.
Grind	ground.	Sting	stung.
Hang	hung, R.	Stink	stunk.

Present.	Past.	Present.	Past.
Hear	heard.	String	strung.
Hold	held.	Sweat	swet, R.
Keep	kept.	Swing	swung.
Lay	laid.	Teach	taught.
Lead	led.	Tell	told.
Leave	left.	Think	thought.
Lend	lent.	Weep	wept.
Lose	lost.	Win	won.
Make	made.	Wind	wound.
Meet	met.	Wring	wrung.

Bit has also *bitten* for the perfect participle, and *cleave* has *clove* or *cloven*. *Ring* has *rang* for the past tense, *sing* has *sang*, *sink* has *sank*, and *spring* has *sprang*. *Hang* is regular when it denotes the execution of a criminal.

3. Such as have a past time independent of the perfect participle. The past tense of this class must not be joined to auxiliaries.

Pres.	Past.	Part.
Arise	arose	arisen.
Awake, R.	awoke	awaked
Bear *	bare	born.
Bear †	bore	borne.
Begin	began	begun.
Blow	blew	blown.
Break	broke	broken.
Choose	chose	chosen.

* To bring forth.
† To carry.

ETYMOLOGY.

Pres.	Past.	Part.
Crow, R.	crew	crowed
Dare, R.	durst	dared
Draw	drew	drawn.
Drive	drove	driven.
Eat	ate	eaten.
Fall	fell	fallen.
Fly	flew	flown.
Forsake	forsook	forsaken.
Freeze	froze	frozen.
Give	gave	given.
Go	went	gone.
Grow	grew	grown.
Know	knew	known.
Lade	laded	laden.
Lie	lay	lain.
Rise	rose	risen.
Rive	rived	riven.
Shake	shook	shaken.
Shear	sheared	shorn.
Slay	slew	slain.
Shew	shewed	shown.
Slide	slid	slidden.
Smite	smote	smitten.
Speak	spoke	spoken.
Steal	stole	stolen.
Strive	strove	striven.
Stride	strode	stridden.
Swear	swore	sworn.
Take	took	taken.

Pres.	Past.	Part.
Tear	tore	torn.
Thrive, R.	throve	thriven.
Throw	threw	thrown.
Tread	trod	trodden.
Wear	wore	worn.
Weave	wove	woven.
Write	wrote	written.

The present tense of *eat* is sometimes used as the past. *Stride* has also *strid* for the perfect participle. *Dare* is regular when it signifies *to defy.*

4. Such as have a past tense independent of the perfect participle, either of which may be used with auxiliaries; the perfect participle must not, however, be put for the past tense.

Pres.	Past.	Part.
Chide	chid	chidden.
Clothe	clothed	clad.
Drink	drank	drunk.
Forget	forgot	forgotten.
Grave	graved	graven.
Hide	hid	hidden.
Hew	hewed	hewn.
Load	loaded	laden.
Mow	mowed	mown.
Ride	rode	ridden.
Saw	sawed	sawn.
Shave	shaved	shaven.
Sow	sowed	sown.
Strike	struck	striken.

ETYMOLOGY.

Pres.	Past.	Part.
Work	wrought	worked.

The following are too irregular to admit of classification: their past tenses must not be joined to auxiliaries.

Pres.	Past.	Part.
Beat	beat	beaten.
Come	came	come.

Am, have, and *be,* are the only auxiliaries that can stand next to a perfect participle.

The following table exhibits the variations of an irregular verb from each class.

	Pres.	Past.	Perf. part.	Imp. part.
1.	Burst	burst	burst	bursting.
	Burstest	burstest	——	——
	Bursts or bursteth	——	——	——
2.	Abide	abode	abode	abidtng.
	Abidest	abodest	——	——
	Abides or abideth	——	——	——
3.	Arise	arose	arisen	arising.
	Arisest	arosest	——	——
	Arises or ariseth	——	——	——
4.	Chide	chid	chidden or chid	chiding.
	Chidest	chidst	——	——
	Chides or chideth	——	——	——

As the terminations *st* and *est* are nearly obsolete, such forms of the verb as *burstest, abodest, arosest,* &c. are seldom met with.

ADVERBS.

An Adverb is a part of speech which is joined to a verb, to shew the manner of its action; to an adjective, to increase, and to another adverb, to modify its signification: as,

To a verb. He reads *well.*

To an adjective. *Extremely* proper.

To another adverb. He reads *remarkably* well.

A LIST OF THE PRINCIPAL ADVERBS.

1. Of number. *Once, twice, thrice,* &c.
2. Of order. *Firstly, secondly, lastly, finally,* &c.
3. Of place. *Here, there, where, elsewhere, whither, hither, thither, upward, downward, whence, hence,* &c.
4. Of time. *Now, already, before, lately, heretofore, henceforward, instantly, presently, immediately, straightway, oft, often, sometimes, soon, seldom, daily, weekly, always, when, then, ever, never, again,* &c.
5. Of quantity. *Much, little, sufficiently, greatly, enough, abundantly,* &c.
6. Of manner or quality. Adverbs of manner or quality are chiefly formed by adding *ly* to adjectives: as, *wise, wisely; foolish, foolishly,* &c.
7. Of doubt. *Perhaps, peradventure, possibly.*
8. Of affirmation. *Verily, truly, undoubtedly, doubtless, certainly, yea, yes, surely, indeed, really,* &c.

9. Of negation or denying. *No, nay, not,* &c.

10. Of interrogation. *How? Wherefore? Whither?*

More, most; better, best; worse, worst; little, less, least, &c. are *adjectives* when they are joined to substantives, but, under any other circumstances, they are *adverbs*.

Some adverbs are compared: as,

Soon, sooner, soonest, &c.

Many adjectives, besides those already noticed, are, by the addition of *ly*, converted into adverbs.

PREPOSITIONS.

Prepositions are used to shew the relations which nouns and pronouns bear to each other: as,

He went *from* London *to* York, and *from* thence *to* Edinburgh.

The principal prepositions are, *of, to, from, by, with, in, into, for, within, without, over, under, through, above, below, between, beneath, up, beyond, except, betwixt, excepting, save, at, near, down, before, behind, off, on, upon, among, after, about, against.*

At is used before villages, towns, and foreign cities: as,

I was *at* Liverpool, *at* Lincoln, *at* Paris.

In is placed before names of countries and principal cities: as,

I live *in* London, *in* England.

CONJUNCTIONS.

Conjunctions connect words and sentences: as,

Two *and* two are four. You are healthy, *because* you are temperate.

The principal conjunctions are, *and, if, because, wherefore, both, as, since, but, unless, or, either, nor, neither, than, yet, lest, notwithstanding, though.*

Some conjunctions correspond to each other: as,

Neither to nor—*neither* he *nor* she.

Though to yet—*though* he was rich, *yet* for, &c.

Whether to or—*whether* he *or* she go.

Either to or—*either* he *or* she will.

As to as—*as* good *as* he.

As to so—*as* the stars, *so* shall thy seed be, &c.

INTERJECTIONS.

Interjections are words that express sudden grief: as, *O! oh! alas!*—contempt: as, *Pish! tush!*—wonder: as, *Ha! really! strange! indeed!*—calling: as, *Hem! ho! soho!*—aversion: as, *Foh! fie! away!*—attention; as, *Lo! behold! hark!*—silence: as, *Hush! hist!*—salutation: as, *Welcome! hail!*

The same word is frequently used in different parts of speech: as,

I will *love* you with an everlasting *love*.

The following examples may perhaps be useful to the learner.

Substantive.

A *calm* after a storm.   It casts a *damp* over us.

Adjective.

A *calm* day.   A *damp* night.

Verb.

We should *calm* our passions.   It will *damp* his ardour.

Substantive.

Better is a *little* with content, &c.   The desire of getting *much*, &c.

Adjective.

A *little* boy.   *Much* money.

Adverb.

He thinks *little*.   I think *much* about it.

IMPERFECT PARTICIPLE.

As a Substantive.

His *singing* was very bad.   His manner of *speaking* is good.

As an Adjective.

A *singing* bird   A *speaking* trumpet.

As a verb.

She was *singing*.   He is *speaking*.

To *walk* in a garden; here walk is a *verb*. He went from *walk* to *walk*; here walk, in both instances, is a *substantive*.

SYNTAX.

Syntax teaches the proper arrangement of words in a sentence.

A sentence is an assemblage of words forming a complete idea, and consists of a *subject*, a *finite verb*, and an *object*.

The subject is that word which denotes the person or thing that is first mentioned in the sentence, or that is the cause of the action, state, or condition.

The object is that word which denotes the person or thing affected by the action of a transitive verb. If the verb be intransitive the sentence does not require an object: as,

Subject.	Verb.	Object.
John	loves	Mary.
Mary	loves	John.
I	instruct	him.
He	instructs	me.
John	sits.	
Mary	walks.	

The subject may be either a *substantive*, a *relative*, or a *nominative personal pronoun*. The object may be represented either by a *substantive* or by an *objective pronoun*.

Sentences are either *simple* or *compound*. They

are also of three kinds: *explicative*, or explaining: *interrogative*, or questioning: *imperative*, or commanding.

A sentence is simple when it contains but one finite verb, and compound when it comprises more than one: as,

    Simp. Time *is* short. Art *is* long.

    Comp. Time *is* short, and art *is* long.

Any collection of words which have no dependence on a finite verb, is a phrase: as,

    The tutor, *by instruction and discipline*, lays the foundation of the pupil's honour. It is, *to say the least of it*, a great disadvantage. The king, *approving the plan*, put it in execution. They set out early, and, *before the close of day*, arrived at the destined place.

When simple sentences are joined together, so as to form but one compound sentence, they are called clauses.

A clause is either *principal* or *parenthetical*.

The principal clause of a sentence is that which contains the assertion or chief subject.

A parenthetical, or secondary clause, is a simple sentence, introduced by a conjunction or other connective word, for the purpose of giving some additional explanation of the principal clause: as,

      Principal.   Parenthetical.

He will not be pardoned, unless he repent.

      Parenthetical.   Principal.

While the bridegroom tarried, they all slumbered and slept.

A principal clause must contain a complete idea, even when separated from the rest of the sentence: as,

>He will not be pardoned. They all slumbered and slept.

A parenthetical clause never conveys a complete sense: as,

>Unless he repent. While the bridegroom tarried.

Words that would occur in two or more clauses, are mostly expressed in the first clause and omitted in the others: as,

>They took away their furniture, *they took away their* clothes, and *they took away their* stock in trade.—They took away their furniture, clothes, and stock in trade.

This omission of words is called an ellipsis. There is scarcely a sentence in which the ellipsis is not used. Great care must be taken, however, not to carry it too far, as we may thereby weaken the force of the sentence, or render our meaning obscure. When the ellipsis is used, the words that are omitted are said to be understood.

The following are examples of the use of the ellipsis. The words in *italics* are those which may with propriety be omitted.

>A man, *a* woman, and *a* child. A house and *a* garden. The sun and *the* moon. The laws of God and *the laws* of man. A delightful garden and *a delightful* orchard. My house and *my* lands. William *who is* king of Great Britain. He regards his word, but thou dost not *regard thy word.*

RULES.

1. Whenever the pronoun *thou* is used as a subject, the verb to which it belongs must end in the personal termination *st* or *est*: as,

Thou love*st* me. Thou walk*est*.

2. When either *he*, *she*, or *it*, or a substantive in the singular number is the subject, the verb takes the personal termination *s* or *es*: as,

He love*s*. She walk*s*. It run*s*. The man talk*s*. The girl learn*s*.

Am, when joined to any of these subjects, changes to *is* in the present tense, and to *was* in the past: as,

He *is* there. She *was* coming. It *is* here.

Shall, will, may, and can, never take *s* or *es*.

3. A verb never takes the personal terminations after the subject *I, we, ye, you, they*, or a plural substantive, nor after two or more singular subjects joined by the conjunction *and*: as,

I *love*. We *walk*. You *run*. They *talk*. The boys *play*. He *and* she s*it*. The man, woman, *and* child *ride*.

Whenever the terminations ought to be rejected, *am* changes to *are* in the present tense, and to *were* in the past, except when the pronoun *I* is the subject: as,

You *were* there. We *are* coming. I *am* here.

4. If subjects of the singular number be joined by *or* or *nor*, the verb will admit the terminations. In this case *is* and *was* must be used, as directed in the second rule: as,

He *or* she come*s*. Neither he *nor* she *is* there.

5. When a verb is used for *commanding, exhorting, entreating,* or *permitting,* it will not take the terminations after any subject; nor when *lest* and *that* are introduced to denote a *caution* or *command:* as,

>Go thou. Do thou go. Let him *walk. Lest* he come. See *that* thou *speak* not to him.

6. A verb, attended by auxiliaries, retains its simple or infinitive form, and the first auxiliary alone takes the terminations, when admissible: as,

>Thou *wilt* love. He *does* walk. She *has* been loved. Thou *mightst* have been hurt.

7. The auxiliaries *may, can, shall,* and *will,* with their variations, *might, could, should,* and *would,* are frequently understood after the conjunctions *if, though, whether, unless, except,* &c. In such case the verb retains its simple or infinitive form, the same as when the auxiliary is expressed.

The general rule is to reject the terminations, whenever the sentence expresses a doubt, or contains a supposition; but whenever a thing is spoken of as positive and certain, the terminations, if required, must be adopted: as,

>If thou *be* afflicted, repine not—*shouldst* be. He will not be clean, unless he *wash* himself—*will* wash himself. If he *do* but touch the mountains.—Positive or certain. Though he *was* a son, yet learned he obedience—we cannot say though he *should be* a son, &c. because it is certain that he was one, or he could not have learned obedience.

Were, when *should* is dropt, is frequently used instead of the infinitive *be:* as,

> No person, unless it *were* given him from above. No person, unless it *be* given, &c. i. e. *should* be given. *Were* he wise, he would not be extravagant; i. e. *Should* he be wise, &c. If he *be* wise.

8. Sometimes a phrase or a clause is the subject of a verb: as,

> *To see the sun*, is pleasant.

If several clauses follow each other, being subjects of the same verb, and if each clause contain a distinct assertion, the verb must be put in the infinitive or simple form. But if the clauses merely explain one another, or describe the same thing throughout, the terminations must be used according to the foregoing rules: as,

> To be temperate in eating and drinking, to use exercise in the open air, and to preserve the mind free from tumultuous emotions, *are* the best preservatives of health.
>
> That warm climates should accelerate the growth of the human body, and shorten its duration, *is* very reasonable to believe.

9. If subjects of different numbers, or if two or more pronouns in the singular number but of different persons be joined by *or* or *nor*; or if *I* or *thou* be in like manner joined to a singular substantive; the verb agrees with that word which stands next to it, and takes or rejects the terminations accordingly.

The first person mostly stands next the verb in preference to the second, the second in preference to the third, and the plural number in preference to the singular: as,

>Either the men or the *boy goes* to day.
>Either the boy or the *men go.*
>Either thou or *I go.*
>Either he or *thou goest.*
>Either the man or *I go.*

10. When the relatives *who, which, what,* and *that,* are used as subjects, the verbs to which they belong must agree in termination with the antecedents, or words for which the relatives stand.

As is sometimes used as a relative: as,

>*Thou* who *lovest* wisdom. *He* that *lives* next door. The *boy* and *girl* who *pass* my door every morning. The *boy* who *passes* my door. The *girl* who *passes* my door. His *words* were *as follow.*

11. The antecedent may be the subject of another verb, as,

>The *man,* who lives next door, *rises* every morning at six.

12. When the relative has two antecedents of different numbers or persons, the verb must agree with that which accords with the sense: as,

>*I* am the instructor who *teach* you; i. e. *I* who teach you am the instructor. I am the *instructor* who teaches you, i. e. the *instructor* who teaches you is I.

13. Every finite verb must have a subject expressed

or understood. When the subject is understood, the verb mostly agrees with some other word in the sentence: as,

He has preserved me, and *can* continue to preserve.

The subject and the antecedent may either of them be discovered, by asking a question with *who* or *what* joined to the verb: as,

The man sees and hears. *Who* sees and hears? The *man*—here *man* is the subject. The man who sees and hears. *Who* sees and hears? The *man*—*man* is therefore antecedent to *who*.

14. The subject is placed after the verb when a question is asked, a command given, a wish expressed, or a supposition made without the conjunction *if;* also when *there* or *here* is joined to an intransitive verb.

Subjects may be generally placed either before or after intransitive verbs: as,

Confidest *thou* in me? Go *thou.* May *he* be happy. Were *he* good he would be happy. Had *I* been there. There was a *man.* Here am *I.* On a sudden appeared the *King*, or the *King* appeared on a sudden.

15. Every substantive and every pronoun must be either the subject or the object of a verb, or belong to a preposition expressed or understood.

[If the pupil supply understood words, he will discover his errors, if there be any; as, you can read better than me [*can*]. *Me* should be *I.* Who did it? Me [*did* it]—*I.* She is as good as him [*is*]—*he.*]

The substantive or pronoun which follows *am* and *be*, or any of their variations, has frequently no agreement with other words, being used merely as a repetition of the subject: as,

>Thou art the *man*. It is *I*.

The verb may be discovered by asking what the subject does: as,

>The man sees and hears. What does the man do? *See* and *hear*.

The object may be discovered by asking a question with *what, who,* or *whom,* joined to the subject and its verb: as,

>John loves Mary. *Whom* does John love? Mary.

16. The objective pronouns *me, him, her, it, us, you, thee,* and *them,* follow transitive verbs, prepositions, and participles of transitive verbs. They are sometimes placed before the verbs which they should follow: as,

>I love *her*. I called on *him*. She is persuading *them*. He loved *her*. *Him* declare I unto you, or I declare *him* unto you. *Him* who committed the offence, thou shouldst *correct*, or thou shouldst correct *him* who committed the offence.

17. *Am* and *be*, in all their variations, take the same sort of pronoun after as before them. *Let* is always followed by an objective: as,

>I am *him*; it should be, I am *he*. Let *him* go.

18. An infinitive verb or a phrase is sometimes the object of a transitive verb: as,

>I acknowledge *that he is right*.

19. If the substantive or pronoun, which stands before *be*, follow a transitive verb, or a preposition, the pronoun that comes after this auxiliary must be objective: as,

 I understand *it* to be *him*. I know the *girl* to be *her*.

20. Some verbs are either transitive or intransitive, according to the sense in which they are used: as,

 They *searched* the house. They searched *for* the house.

21. A transitive verb must not have an object after it introduced by a preposition, nor must an intransitive verb have an object without a preposition: as,

 Trans. I must premise *with* three circumstances. *With* ought to be rejected.

 Intrans. I mostly *lay* in bed late. It should be *lie*.

 [*Lay* is the past tense of the intransitive verb *lie*: as, I *lay* in bed late yesterday. But when *lay* is used in the present tense, it is transitive, and has *lain* or *laid* for the perfect participle: as, Should I lay the books down? I *laid* the books down. I have *lain* the books down.]

22. *Am* and *be* must not, in any of their variations, be joined to perfect participles of intransitive verbs: as,

 Whose number *was* amounted to fifty—*had* amounted.

23. Infinitive verbs may depend upon substantives and adjectives, as well as upon finite verbs: as,

 He has a *desire* to learn. He is *desirous* to learn.

24. *To* is seldom used when the infinitive follows the verbs *bid, dare, need, make, see, hear, feel, do,*

say, shall, will, may, can, know, have, observe, and *perceive:* as,

> To *see* so many *to* make so little conscience of sin.
> I *bid* him *to* do it. I *do to* love. I *did to* walk.
> In all these examples *to* should be omitted.

25. To represent an action or event in an active state, or as going on at the time referred to, the imperfect participle must be joined to *am* or *be,* or to some of their variations: as,

> I *am playing.* I *was playing.* We *were walking.*
> I have *been walking.*

26. The simple form of the verb and the perfect participle, merely declare or affirm the existence of an action or event at the time referred to: as,

> I *play.* I *do play.* I *walked.* I *did walk.*

27. *Have,* as an auxiliary, cannot be joined to a perfect participle when any thing intervenes to break the connexion between the finishing of an action, or event, and the time at which we are speaking, nor when a past time is either expressed or understood.

We cannot say—Mary, queen of Scots, *has been* remarkable for her beauty and misfortunes—because her death breaks the connexion between the events of her life and the present time. Nor can we say—Cicero *has written* poems which are lost—because the circumstance of the loss limits the event to a past time; that is, the poems have not come down to us; they cannot, therefore, have any connexion with the present period.

It is improper to say—In my last letter I *have given* you all the information in my power—because the last letter has no connexion with that which I am now writing. He *has* arrived last Wednesday—is also improper, because a past time is expressed.

Have should be used when nothing arises to break the connexion between a past and finished action and the present time.

We can say—Mary, queen of Scots, *has been* dead nearly two hundred and fifty years—because nothing intervenes to break the connexion between the period or circumstance of her death and the time at which we are speaking. Cicero *has written* orations—is correct, because the orations are still in existence. In my present letter I *have given* you all the information in my power—is equally correct, because the information is contained in the letter that I am now writing. The expressions—I *have been;* I *have loved;* and those of a similar nature, are correct, because they are evidently connected with a present time. He *has arrived*—is proper, because no past time is denoted.

The length of time between the completion of an action or event, and the time at which we are speaking, is of no consideration, provided there be no interruption. We may say with propriety—The world *has been* created 5835 years. But we cannot say— It is 5835 years since the world *has been* created—because here are two unconnected circumstances, though they have relation to the same event.—The latter example properly comes under rule 30.

If there be any interruption, or separation, with

regard to time, or any allusion to a past period, no matter how short the time, all connexion with the present is at an end: as,

> I *was* there a minute *ago*—not, I *have been* there a minute ago.

28. In stating events that are limited to a past period, the past tense, or the perfect participle without *have*, must be used: as,

> Mary, queen of Scots, *was* remarkable for her beauty and misfortunes. Cicero *wrote* poems which are lost. In my last letter I *gave* you all the information in my power. He *arrived* last Wednesday.

29. In representing events that transpired before a past period, *had* must be joined to a perfect participle: as,

> Mary, queen of Scots, *had been* a prisoner in England many years *before* she was beheaded. Cicero *had been* famous for his oratory long before he made his celebrated accusation of Catiline. In my last letter I *thought* I *had given* you all the information in my power.

30. If actions or events, which in point of time relate to each other, occur at different periods, *have* or *had* cannot be joined to more than one participle; and when *have* or *had* is not used, the verbs must be in different tenses: as,

> The Lord *gave* and the Lord *has* taken away. I *tell* you he *has* been there. I *told* you he *had* been there. It *is* 5835 years since the world *was* created.

31. If actions or events, that depend upon each other, be represented as taking place at the same time, the verbs must be in the same tense, and each participle must take *have* or *had*, if at all required: as,

> He *came* into the room the moment I *arrived*.
> John will *have earned* his wages when he *has finished* his work.

32. If the action or event, denoted by an infinitive verb, take place before that of the finite verb, *to have* must be joined to the perfect participle, instead of using the infinitive in its simple form: as,

> From his biblical knowledge, he *appears to have studied* the scriptures with attention.

33. When the action or event of an infinitive verb occurs at or after the time of the action or event of the finite verb, the simple form of the infinitive must be used: as,

> I intend *to write*. I intended *to write*.

The infinitive that follows a verb in the present tense must also be used after the past tense of the same verb, when the same actions are represented.

[Therefore when the finite verb is in the past tense, reduce it to the present, and, whatever form the infinitive assumes, let that form be retained: as, I expect *to find* him. I expected *to find* him. I shall *have been* there. I should *have been* there. When two finite verbs, which in point of time relate to each other, have an infinitive following the latter, both finite verbs must be reduced to the present tense: as, I *fear* I *shall lose* it. I *feared* I *should lose* it.]

34. Such things as undergo no change, must have their verbs in the present tense, without regard to the tenses of other verbs: as,

> The doctor *said* that fevers always *produce* thirst.
> The bishop *declared* that virtue *is* always advantageous.

35. When the perfect participle of a transitive verb is joined to *am* or *be* in any of their variations, the object is put as the subject, and the subject, with a preposition, is placed after the participle: as,

> *She* loves me.   *They* called us.
> I *am* loved by *her*.   We *are* called by *them*.

Sometimes participles of *intransitive* verbs are used with *am* and *be;* but the participle is then rendered transitive by being joined to a preposition, forming a kind of compound word: as,

> She might have thought of me.
> I might have *been* thought *of* by her.

36. Personal pronouns must be of the same number and gender as the substantives for which they stand: as,

> The *King* put on his robes before *he* entered the house.   The *men* came, but *they* went away.

37. Definitive adjectives must be of the same number and gender as the substantives to which they relate: as

> The King had put on *his* robes.   The King and the Queen had put on *their* robes.

When two or more substantives are referred to separately, the definitive adjectives must be in the singular number: as,

> John or James is the man, for each regards *his* duty.

38. The relative always stands before the verb. *Whom* is used instead of *who*, when the relative is not the subject of a verb: as,

    The man *whom* you saw last night called this morning.

39. A substantive and its pronoun cannot be subjects of the same verb: as,

    The *man* whom you saw this morning *he* called last night.—*He* ought to be rejected.

40. When *who* is used in a question, it requires a nominative pronoun in the answer; *whom* requires an objective: as,

    Who gave you that book? *He* that called yesterday. Of *whom* did he buy it? Of *him* that lives at the corner.

41. " *They* stands for a substantive already expressed, and should never be used till the substantive be mentioned:" as,

    They who study grammar. It should be—*those* who study grammar.

42. *Soever* is mostly separated from the word to which it belongs: as,

    On *whichsoever* side. It should be—On *which* side *soever*.

43. Every adjective and every genitive noun belongs to a substantive expressed or understood: as,

    This [subject] is a *great* [subject] as well as an *important* subject. *This* book is *John's* [book].

44. *This, that,* and *another,* are joined to singular substantives. *My, thy, his, our, your, their,* and *any,*

belong to substantives either of the singular or plural number. *These, those, some, other, all,* and *such,* are placed before plurals. *Mine, thine, hers, ours, yours, theirs,* and *others,* are used when the substantive is understood: as,

>*This* book. *Those* books. *Another* man. *Other* men. This house is *yours* [your house.] This book is *mine* [my book.] that is *hers.* [her book.]

45. *Each, every,* and *either,* are singular. *Each* is used when two objects are considered in the same light; *either* denotes only one of two objects; *every* considers objects singly, but includes them all: as,

>*Each* boy took his hat; i. e. they both took their hats. *Either* he or she took it. *Every* one of you; i. e. all of you.

46. *Another* should be used with *one,* and *some* with *other:* as,

>From *one* to *another.* At *some* time or *other.*

47. The adjective is sometimes placed after the substantive, and is frequently separated from it by a verb: as,

>A boy *studious.* A girl *attentive* to her lessons. Error is *human.* This *apple* is *ripe.*

48. Verbs, joined together by conjunctions, must be in the same tense, unless the subject be repeated.

Pronouns, joined by conjunctions, must be of the same kind: as,

>He *reads* and *writes* well. *Did* he not tell thee his fault and *entreat* thee to forgive him?

Him and *I,* should be either *him* and *me,* or *he* and *I.*

49. The comparative degree and the definitive adjective *other*, require *than* after them, and *such* requires *as*: as,

> Greater *than* I. No other *than* he. *Such as* I have, give I unto thee.

50. A pronoun after *than* or *as* is either the subject or the object of a verb understood, or belongs to a preposition: as,

> Greater than I [*am.*] No other than he [*is.*] She loved him more than [*she loved*] me. The sentiment is well expressed by Plato, but much better by Solomon than [*by*] him.

51. If one adverb of time or place and another of quality or manner attend upon a single verb, the adverb of time or place must be set before the verb, and that of quality or manner must be placed after it; as,

> He every *where* declared *publicly* his intention.

52. A single adverb is mostly set between a single auxiliary and its verb; but if there be two auxiliaries, the adverb is placed between them.

" If there be two adverbs and two auxiliaries, the adverbs will be intermixed with the auxiliaries:" as,

> Folly has *always* exposed her author. He should *certainly* have come. I have *always* been *much* embarrassed by these inconveniences.

53. In a sentence wherein *am* or *be*, in any of their variations, is joined to the perfect participle of a transitive verb, the single adverb is mostly placed next to

the participle, without regard to the number of auxiliaries: as,

>He will be *uncommonly* agitated. I might have been *better* informed.

It is impossible to give invariable rules for placing the adverbs; the sense of the passage must be our chief guide. It may, however, be taken as a general rule, that adverbs must occupy that part of the sentence wherein the words and phrases, for which they stand, would be placed: as,

>Adverb. She loves him *sincerely*.
>
>Subs. She loves him with *sincerity*.
>
>Adj. She loves him with *sincere* love.
>
>Adv. Thou art *naturally blessed* with a good memory.
>
>Adj. Thy good memory is a *natural blessing*.
>
>Adv. We must not expect study to be *always* agreeable.
>
>Adj. We must not expect study to be attended with *continued agreeableness*.

54. Adverbs must never be used for adjectives, nor adjectives for adverbs: as,

>Adj. He lives in a *manner agreeable* to the dictates of religion.
>
>Adv. He lives *agreeably* to the dictates of religion.

55. When several genitive nouns come together, connected by conjunctions, the genitive *'s* is added only to the last, except when a particular emphasis is required: as,

>John and Eliza's books. They are John's as well as Eliza's books.

56. The genitive can never be an antecedent to a relative. It is frequently placed before imperfect participles; the participle is then, however, a substantive in signification: as,

> A great deal depends upon a pupil's *applying* himself; i. e. a pupil's application.

57. The genitive noun must not be separated from its substantive by an intervening phrase: as,

> She praised the farmer's, *as she called him*, wisdom.

58. Two negatives, i. e. denials, must not come together, unless it be intended to produce an affirmative: as,

> I can*not* by *no* means. It should be—by *any* means. *Nor* did they *not* perceive him; i. e. they did perceive him.

59. Double comparatives and superlatives must be avoided: as,

> A *worser* conduct—*worse*. A *more* better boy—*more* is superfluous.

60. The articles *a* and *an* are joined to words in the singular number only; *the* is added to words in both numbers: as,

> *A* man. *An* eagle. *The* man. *The* men.

61. *A* is used before a word beginning with a consonant, the long sound of *u*, and *w* and *y*. *An* is prefixed to a word beginning with a vowel or a silent *h*, and even when the *h* is sounded, if the accent be on the second syllable of the word before which the article stands: as,

> *A* house. *A* unicorn. *A* whisper. *A* youth.
> *An* egg. *An* hour. *An* heroical action.

62. The articles are omitted before substantives comprehending a whole species, and before minerals, metals, arts, and sciences: as,

The man—means some particular man; but *man*, without the article, denotes all mankind. *The* gold, *the* Astronomy—mean some particular pieces of gold, or a book upon astronomy.

63. The interjections *O! oh!* and *ah!* require *me* after them.

MISCELLANEOUS RULES AND OBSERVATIONS.

Whenever such substantives as *meeting, parliament, people, multitude,* &c. comprising many in one, are used as subjects, the verbs to which they belong may take or reject the personal termination *s* or *es*, yet not without regard to the import of the words as implying numbers.

It is and *it was* have often a plural after them: as,
   It is *they*. It was the *men*.

An imperfect participle of a transitive verb, preceded by an article, must be followed by the preposition *of; having* is an exception: as,
   The preaching *of* Christ.

There is frequently used merely to introduce a verb: as,
   There was a man.

It is sometimes used without reference to a substantive: as,
   It rains.

A substantive, when joined to a preposition, has no effect upon the verb, except through the medium of a relative: as,

> The general, *with* his *officers*, *has* applied for redress.

This and *these* stand for persons or things that are first mentioned, or that are nearest the speaker; *that* and *those* for such as are last mentioned, or that are farthest off: as,

> *This* book is mine, *that* is yours.

When *each*, *either*, or *neither* is put without a substantive, the verb that follows will take *s* or *es*: as,

> *Each* of these men earn*s*, &c. *Either* of them suit*s* me.

An article is sometimes placed between a substantive and its adjective: as,

> So bad *a* temper.

A is sometimes used with a plural substantive: as,

> *A* few *men*.

When two or more substantives are joined by *and*, with an article prefixed only to the first, they denote the same person or thing. If, therefore, we wish to represent different persons or things, the article must be repeated before each substantive: as,

> The secretary and treasurer *is* here. The secretary and *the* treasurer *are* here. I bought a black and white cow, and paid twelve pounds each for them—a black and *a* white cow.

The first person is preferred to the second, and the second to the third: as,

> *You*, *he*, and *I* have *our* objections.

A preposition should never be separated from the relative to which it belongs: as,

Whom did he go w*ith?* It should be—*with whom* did he go?

" *That* is generally used after the superlative degree and after the adjective *same:*" as,

He is the *best* man *that*, &c. She is the *same* person *that*, &c.

Pronouns must never be joined to substantives: as,

Give me *them* books. It should be—*those* books.

" Two prepositions in the same construction are improper:" as,

A match *between* ten boys of one school *against* ten boys, &c. It should be—*and* ten boys, &c.

Ever, not *never*, should be used with *so;* as,

Be it *ever* so true.

In most cases the genitive noun may be avoided by a different arrangement of the sentence: as,

Man's happiness—the happiness of man.

Most adjectives of two syllables, and all above that number, form their degrees of comparison by *more* and *most*. *Most* is sometimes affixed to a word: as,

Under*most*, upper*most*.

The adjectives *enow* and *enough* always follow their substantives. *Enow* denotes number; *enough* expresses quantity: as,

He has got cherries *enow*. He has drunk *enough*.

Farther applies to distance, *further* to quantity.

Whosoever, whichsoever, and the like, are compound relative pronouns, and relate to an understood antecedent, signifying any person.

Self is a substantive, but is mostly joined to a pronoun, or a definitive adjective: as,

    Myself, thyself, himself.

It is frequently used when the gender is unknown: as,

    It is a fine child.

Whose is frequently applied to neuter substantives.

No is sometimes improperly used instead of *not:* as,

    I cannot tell whether he will go or *no* [go.] It should be —*not*.

The article *an* must not be placed before a vowel having the sound of a consonant: as,

    Such *a* one [*won*]—not *an* one.

The is used before the names of *seas*, *rivers*, and *ships*, and before proper substantives when used in the plural number: as,

    The Thames. *The* Irish sea. *The* William. *The* Charleses. *The* Indies.

When the name of a person and his profession come together, the name, and not the profession, must be converted into a genitive noun: as,

    I bought them at *Albin's*, the bookseller.

News is used in the singular only; *means* is used in both numbers.

One instead of *I* is frequently used as the subject of a verb: as,

    One is apt to think much of it.

It is improper to repeat the same idea, even by different words: as,

    To return *back*. To return *again*. To fall *down*. To rise *up*. They have a mutual likeness to *each other.* To enter *in.* To restore *back.* First *of all.* Last *of all.* I took some cream and sugar, and put them *both* into the tea. I called on James and we *both* took a walk. I searched all the rooms *throughout.*—Each word in *italics* is the repetition of an idea that has been already expressed.

The ellipsis should never be used when it would occasion an impropriety: as,

Beautiful fields and trees. It should be—beautiful fields and *fine* trees. A house and orchard. It should be—a house and *an* orchard.

The date and direction of a letter are elliptical: as,

This letter was written in London, *on* June *the* 9th,
[*in the year* 1831.

This letter is to be delivered to
Mr. Smith, *who lives at*
No. 9, Chandos-Street, *in*
LONDON.

PUNCTUATION.

COMMA.

Phrases must be marked off by commas: as,

If, *from any internal cause,* a man's peace of mind be destroyed, &c.

When two or more adjectives belong to one substantive, a comma must be placed after each adjective, except the last: as,

A sober, honest, and industrious man.

Two or more subjects belonging to the same verb require a comma after each subject; two or more verbs belonging to the same subject require a comma after each verb; and two or more adverbs qualifying the same verb require a comma after each adverb: as,

> The husband, wife, and children suffered.
> We may exhort, comfort, and admonish.
> He acted wisely, prudently, and discreetly.

A comma is not required when two words only are joined by a conjunction: as,

> The husband *and* wife suffered. We may exhort *and* comfort. He acted wisely *and* prudently.

When words follow each other in pairs, a comma must be placed between each pair: as,

> Truth is fair and artless, simple and sincere, uniform and constant.

An expression in the form of a command, quotation, or direct address, must be marked off by a comma: as,

> I say unto all, *watch*. Plutarch calls lying, *the vice of fools*. *Sir*, your most obedient.

When a verb is understood, a comma ought to supply its place: as,

> To err is human, to forgive, [*is*] divine.

Words that mean the same person or thing must be separated by commas: as,

> The gulf, or bay, &c. Henry Brougham, Lord Brougham. Thomas Smith, *Secretary*.

Emphatic words, and words that imply opposition, must be pointed off by commas: as,

> — captain, you, even you, &c. He was learned, but not pedantic.

Parenthetical clauses must be separated from principal clauses by commas: as,

> *While the bridegroom tarried,* they all slumbered and slept.

SEMICOLON.

When principal clauses come together, they must be parted by semicolons: as,

> He that loveth pleasure shall be a poor man; he that loveth wine and oil shall not be rich. The orator speaks the truth plainly to his hearers; he awakens them; he excites their attention.

Even if the verb and the subject of a principal clause be understood, a semicolon must be used: as,

> — we see deep humility, but not loathsome abjectedness; [*we see*] sincere repentance, but not agonizing horror.

Care must be taken to place the semicolon so as not to separate parenthetical clauses and phrases from their principal clauses: as,

> *The advantages,* according to reason, which arise from the rising and falling of the tides, *are great*; by their means, the streams of rivers being checked, *the bed of the river becomes deeper,* and ships of the largest burden are enabled to sail up their channels with safety.— *The advantages are great,* though it conveys no satisfactory meaning, is a principal clause, being complete and independent in grammatical construction, and forms the leading member,

or that on which the other members depend. The same remarks apply to *the bed of the river becomes deeper.*

COLON.

When a complete and finished sentence, either simple or compound, is followed by an additional remark, giving a further explanation of the foregoing idea, such remark must be pointed off by a colon : as,

>Study to acquire the habit of thinking : *no study is so important.* It is the prerogative of wise men to conquer envy : *merit gives it birth, and merit destroys it.*

Similitudes are parted by colons : as,

>As an ill air may endanger a good constitution : so may a place of ill example endanger a good man.

A colon is used before a direct quotation : as,

>Remember this ancient maxim : *know thyself.* He was often heard to say : *I have done with the world.*

When several semicolons follow each other, a colon may be placed before the last clause.

PERIOD.

When a simple sentence is complete in itself, or when several clauses come together, forming a complete idea, it must be marked by a period : as,

>Fear God. Honour the King. Fear God and

honour the King. The Supreme Being changes not, either in his desire to promote our happiness, or in the plan of his operations.

There are many cases wherein the sense alone can determine the places of the points; as may be seen by the following examples :

    Gate, be thou open; to nobody be shut.
    Gate, be thou open to nobody; be shnt.
    I say unto thee, this day thou shalt be with me in paradise.
    I say unto thee this day, thou shalt be with me in paradise.

The dash [—] is used when a sentence suddenly breaks off and turns to another subject. It ought never to be used with the other points.

The interrogative point [?] is placed at the end of a question.

The exclamation point [!] is used after an exclamatory sentence, or interjection.

The parenthesis ( ) encloses an additional remark thrown into a sentence.

The apostrophe ['] points out the omission of a letter in a word.

The hyphen [-] is used to connect words together. It is also used at the end of a line when a word is divided.

The section [§] and the paragraqh [¶] are chiefly used in old books to point out the subdivisions of a discourse.

The quotation [" "] is placed at each end of a borrowed passage.

Brackets [ ] enclose a word, phrase, or sentence, to be particularly noticed.

An index [☞], in old books, points out a remarkable passage.

A brace } unites three poetical lines, or several common terms in prose.

The asterisk [*], obelisk [†], parallels [∥], and letters of the alphabet, lead to notes at the bottom of the page.

CAPITALS.

The following words should begin with capitals:

The first word of every composition, paragraph, and line in poetry; after a note of interrogation, if the question form a complete sentence; of a quotation beginning with *as;* and the first word after every period.

The names or appellations of the Deity; all proper names and adjectives derived from them; words denoting great events; those which denote the subjects of discourse when they are first introduced, and all emphatic words. The pronoun *I* and the interjection *O* must be capitals.

PROSODY.

Prosody teaches the true pronunciation of words, and the measure of verse.

> [Rules for pronunciation have too many exceptions to be of any great use. Perhaps the exercises in the second part may afford some assistance to the learner.]

Poetry consists of two kinds; rhyme, and blank verse.

When the last word or syllable in a line, corresponds in sound with the last word or syllable in another, it is called rhyme; when this is not the case, it is called blank verse.

DIRECTIONS FOR COMPOSITION.

Use only such words as belong to the language. Avoid all low words and phrases. Be careful to select words that will clearly express your meaning. Never use words or phrases that belong to particular professions, unless you are writing upon those subjects. Supply words that are wanting. Never use the same word oftener than you can help; be careful, however, not to run into the opposite extreme, but if the sense require it, repeat the word without hesitation.

Employ no more words than are absolutely necessary, for one useless word may injure, if not destroy, the effect of a whole sentence.

Phrases and clauses that are nearly related, should be as close to each other as possible: above all, let the relative be near its antecedent.

If the sentence consist of several members, let that clause which contains the chief subject be either first or last; never in the middle. Let the last clause be the most weighty.

Attend to the sense rather than to the sound. Let your sentences be so constrncted as to read as smoothly as possible; but let your style be bold, clear, and simple. Fine words seldom please, because very few understand them. Good sense, in plain language, is sure to gain approbation.

SYNTACTICAL EXERCISES.

The exercises are numbered to correspond to the rules.

1. Thou should come. Will thou stay.

2. He ride. It sink. The man speak. The moon shine.

3. They stays. I loves you. They comes here. The bells rings. Horses gallops. Sorrows, like a flood, overwhelms me. Some boys, from not having a knowledge of grammar, writes incorrectly. The sun, the moon, and the stars, shines. He and she was walking.

4. He or Thomas were there. Either he or she go to town to day. The man or the woman bring it. Neither he nor she like me.

5. Do thou lettest him go. Do thou entreatest him. Mind, lest thou fallest. See that he speaks not to him. I will retire lest he sees me. Let him stay, lest the darkness of the night overtakes him.

6. He do loves me. Thou did walkest. James do reads well.

7. I will call though he drives me out of the house. If thou callest upon him, he will tell thee. Whether thou goest or not, it makes but little difference. Except the Lord keeps the house, the watchman waketh but in vain. Was I in your place I would go. If I was he I would have it. Was there no difference, there would be no choice.

Though he were rich, yet for our sakes he became poor. Though he were divinely inspired, and spake therefore the oracles of God with authority; though he were well endued with supernatural powers, yet in compliance with the way in which human nature is usually wrought upon, he reasoned.

8. To write well are pleasing. To be of a pure and humble mind, to exercise benevolence towards others, to cultivate piety towards God, is the sure means of becoming peaceful and happy. To be carnally minded are death. To be spiritually minded are life eternal.

9. He or they walks to town. Henry and I intends being there. William or I is the person.

10. The man who live here. He that make long speeches. I who teaches you. Blessed is the man who walk in Wisdom's ways. I mean he that sing so well.

11. The man who called say he wishes to see you. Those who pretend the greatest friendship, is the first to desert us in adversity.

13. If we take them from him would be unjust. These we have extracted from an author of undoubted credit, and are the same that were practised, &c. Virtue supports in adversity and it moderates in prosperity.

14. Thou confidest in me? Thou go. You will come?

15. The books, though they were sent, they never arrived. Man, though he has a great variety of thoughts, and such from which others as well as himself might receive profit and delight, yet they are all locked within his own breast.

16. He beats I. She ran against he. They called on she. Have you bought they? Whom ye ignorantly worship, he declare I unto you.

17. I am sure it was him. It was not me that blotted the book.

19. I know it to be he. I understood it to be she. We at first took the woman to be she.

21. I must premise with three circumstances. To ingratiate with some by traducing others, indicates a base mind. He sleeps it well. He will one day repent him of indulgencies so unwarrantable.

22. From which we are greatly swerved. It was ceased long since. He was entered into a conspiracy against his master.

24. Bid him to do it. He need not to make such a noise. Make him to do it.

27. Next Midsummer I shall be at school five years. I have compassion on the multitude, for they continue with me three days. He was, to the present time, regular in his attendance.

28. I have been there yesterday. I have seen him last week. The feudal laws have been degrading. The Druidical priests have claimed great privileges. The reign of George the Third has been a long reign. William the Norman has conquered England. I have heard him preach last year. The ancient Britons have been great idolaters. He has lately lost an only son.

29. George the Third has been afflicted many years before he died. I have breakfasted before he arrived. He that was dead sat up. He has formerly been regular in his attendance.

30. I have given him it, but he has returned it. It is 765 years since England has been conquered by William the First.

31. He had come into the room the moment I arrived. I have been in London a year, and saw the King but once. From the progress he has made, he appears to study grammar some time.

32. From his knowledge of grammar, he seems to study that science attentively. From what I have seen of him, he seems to make himself well acquainted with the subject.

33. Last week I intended to have written. His sickness was so great that I often feared he would have died. There were two circumstances that made it necessary for them to have lost no time. History painters would have found * it difficult to have invented such a species of beings.

34. The master declared that education was an important subject. The preacher assured us that religion alone could make us happy. The lecturer said that Britain was an island.

36. Can any one on his entrance into the world be fully secure that they shall not be deceived? Take handfuls of ashes from the furnace, and let Moses sprinkle it towards heaven. The mind of man cannot be long without some food to nourish the activity of his thoughts.

37. Answer not a fool according to their folly. I do not think any one should incur censure for being tender of their reputation. The wheel has killed another man, who is the sixth that has lost their lives, by this means.

---

* In reducing *would* to its past tense, in order to determine the form of the infinitive, *have* will be necessarily dropped; if, therefore, in again rendering *would* into the past tense, a past and finished action be represented, *have* with the perfect participle must be restored, agreeably to rule 27; but the infinitive *to invent* must retain its simple form: as, History painters will *find* it difficult *to invent*—History painters *would have found* it difficult *to invent*.

The adoption or rejection of *have*, when it would occur in a series of verbs without the preposition *to*, must be determined by rule 27, rather than by the directions given in rule 33.

38. The man who you sent called this morning. I am he who you have insulted. The Being who I serve is eternal.

39. The King he is beloved by his subjects. Such persons who instead of doing good, they are perpetually intent upon doing mischief.

40. Who is there? Me. Who brought the books? Him that lives at the bookseller's. Of whom did he buy them? Of he that lives in the market-place.

45. There are lamps on either side the chimney-piece. He may walk on each side the road. There was a large party, and either seat was full.

48. He loves and feared him. Anger glances into the breast of a wise man, but will rest only in the bosom of fools. Him and I walked home together. He and her staid late last night.

49. He is a much better boy then John. No other man but he.

51, 52, 53. He was pleasing not often. He loved her sincerely. We should not be overcome totally by present events. He unaffectedly and forcibly spoke, and was heard attentively by the assembly. Not only he found her employed, but pleased and tranquil also. We always should prefer our duty to our pleasure. The heavenly bodies are in motion perpetually.

54. He is a true good man. We had scarce got there. I can never think so mean of him. He defines this word agreeable to the common reading. It is upon an entire new plan. He is not only honest, but real good.

55. Thompson's and Smith's library. Bring me John's and James's books. Smith's, Pain's, and Robertson's shop.

58. I have not got nothing. He has not given me none. He has not received no money, nor no advice upon the subject. Neither at the present nor at no other time.

59. It is the most finest poem you ever read. She is the most beautifullest girl I ever saw. This is a worser than the other. We could not have a more beautifuller day.

62 Reason was given to a man but denied to the brutes. We must act our parts with the constancy, though reward of our conduct be distant. Who breaks a butterfly upon a wheel? This day is salvation come to this house, forasmuch as he is the son of Abraham. The fire, the air, the earth, the water, are four elements of philosophers.

EXERCISES IN PUNCTUATION.

I remember with gratitude his love and services. His work is in many respects very imperfect. Syntax when applied to grammar relates to the arrangement of words. I shall therefore give you all the information in my power. He was a brave wise and pious man. She was a woman gentle sensible well-educated and religious.

The husband wife and child suffered extremely. His knowledge his experience his sagacity rendered him master of his subject. He is alternately supported by his father his uncle and his elder brother. The preacher advises exhorts and comforts. He was loved esteemed and respected. The man acted prudently steadily and cautiously.

Truth is fair and artless simple and sincere uniform and constant. Sir your most obedient. Plutarch calls lying the vice of fools. William King of Great Britain. John Percy treasurer. He was learned but not pedantic positive but not supercilious. Vices like shadows towards the evening of life grow great and monstrous.

Straws swim upon the surface pearls lie at the bottom. We are come into the world too late to produce any thing new nature and life are pre-occupied and description and sentiment have long since been exhausted.

Do not flatter yourself with the hope of perfect happiness there is no such thing in the world. Remember this ancient maxim know thyself. The Scriptures represent the Deity in these words GOD is love.

Fear GOD Honour the King Truth is the basis of every virtue Every deviation from veracity is criminal The latin tongue is now called a dead language because it is not spoken as the mother tongue of any nation.

Climate soil laws customs food and other accidental differences have produced an astonishing variety in the complexion features manners and faculties of the human race.

While yet my Hector still survives I see
My father mother brethren all in thee.

Ulysses was a wise eloquent cautious and intrepid hero. Exercise ferments the humours casts them into their proper channels throws off redundances and assists nature in her operations.

When the Romans attacked on all sides by the barbarians were reduced to the necessity of defending the centre of their empire they abandoned Great Britain as well as several other of the distant provinces the island thus left to itself became a prey to the nations inhabiting the shores of the Baltic who having first destroyed the ancient inhabitants and for a long time reciprocally annoyed each other established several sovereignties in the southern part of the island called England which at length were united under Egbert into one kingdom.

EXERCISES IN COMPOSITION.

Supply words that are wanting.

He bought a red and white cow, and paid twelve pounds each for them. He shot a wild and tame pigeon. He lives between the red and white houses. He has left his grammar and spelling book. I gave him a brass and steel pen. He exchanged it for an orange and apple. They received, by post, a letter and newspaper. We passed a carriage, coach, and waggon. He built the bridge and church.

Consider the works of nature and art. He is composing a work on vegetables and animals. He is fond of writing and reading. He took an account of the stock in trade and furniture. It is the book you gave me I have lost. It was at the time he lost the greater part of his fortune, and sufferd severely from sickness. The horse he rode that day is worth fifty pounds. These are the things we possess and claim. I saw the horse he bought last Wednesday. This is the book she sent me.

Threats nor promises could induce him to accept it. He has an elegant house and gardens. A large city and river. The cathedral contains a fine organ and altar-piece. This town is famous for its stately palace and cathedral. The anxious man is the votary of riches; the negligent, of pleasure. We must guard against too great severity, and facility of manners. It will either produce great gain or loss. Many men, and even women, attend those places. The country possesses a changeable climate and soil. He is not only sensible but religious too. By presumption and vanity we provoke enmity and contempt. He is temperate, disinterested, benevolent; an ornament to his family, and credit to his profession.

Reject useless words.

The red and the white cow is in the field. A black and a white magpie. The gulf, or the bay, is very dangerous. The mansion, or the house, in which he lives. The academy, or the school, of which he is a pupil. In the town, or rather the village, where I was visiting, there is a great natural curiosity. These rules are addressed only to the intelligent and the attentive. A man of virtue is an honour to his country, he is a glory to humanity, he is a satisfaction to himself, and he is a benefactor to the whole world.

Friendship is that peculiar relation which is formed by consent and which is formed by harmony of minds and which is formed by mutual esteem and reciprocal tenderness and affection. Religion is the daughter of heaven, it is the parent of all our virtues and it is the guardian of all our pleasures. It is observed of the northen nations, that they do not open the mouth sufficiently for the distinct articulation: and the reason given, why they do not open the mouth sufficiently, is, that the coldness of the air confirms a habit of keeping the mouth as close as possible.

Use such words as will clearly express your meaning, and avoid all ambiguous expressions.

When our friendship is considered, how is it possible that I should not grieve for his loss?

The eagle killed the hen and ate her in her own nest.

Solomon the son of David, who built the temple of Jerusalem, was the richest monarch that reigned over the Jewish people. All words, which are signs of complex ideas, may furnish matter of mistake and cavil Lysias promised to his father, never to abandon his friends. Things new and old.

Sextus the Fourth was, if I mistake not, a great collector of books, at least.

The Romans understood liberty, at least, as well as we.

Phrases and clauses, that are nearly related, should be as near to each other as possible; above all, let the relative be near its antecedent.

[*The phrases and clauses in italics are those which are misplaced.*]

The English are naturally fanciful, and *are very often disposed*, by that gloominess and melancholy of temper which is so frequent in our nation, to many wild notions to which others are not liable.

It is folly to pretend to arm ourselves against the accidents of life, *by heaping up treasures*, which nothing can protect us against, but the good Providence of our heavenly Father.

Thus I have fairly given you, *sir*, my own opinion, *as well as that of a great majority of both houses here* relating to this weighty affair.

From a habit of saving time and paper, *which they have acquired at the university*, they write in so diminutive a manner, with such frequent blots and interlineations, that they are not able to go on without perpetual hesitations, or extemporary expletives.

Though our brother is upon the rack, *as long as we ourselves are at ease*, our senses will never inform us of what he suffers.

The minister who grows less by elevation, *like a*

little statue upon a mighty pedestal, will always have his jealousy strong about him.

We shall now endeavour, *with clearness and precision,* to describe the provinces once united under their sway.

Are these designs which any man, who is born a Briton, in any circumstances, in any situation, *ought to be ashamed or afraid,* to avow?

A great stone that I happened to find, *after a long search,* by the sea shore served me for an anchor.

The emperor was so intent on the establishment of his absolute power in Hungary, that he exposed the empire doubly to desolation and ruin *for the sake of it.*

We no where meet with a more glorious and pleasing shew in nature, than what appears in the heavens at the rising and setting of the sun, *which is wholly made up of those different stains of light, that shew themselves in clouds of a different situation.*

This work in its full extent, being now afflicted with an asthma, and finding the power of life gradually declining, he had no longer courage to undertake.

Instead of being able to employ troops trained to skill in arms, and to military subordination, *by regular discipline,* monarchs were obliged to depend on such forces as their vassals conducted to their standard in consequence of their milirary tenures.

God heapeth favours on his servants *ever liberal and faithful.*

At least my own private letters leave room for a politician, well versed in matters of this nature, to suspect as much, *as a penetrating friend of mine tells me.*

PARSING.

Parsing is an exercise wherein the learner separately examines each word in a sentence, tracing its various modifications, and the relation which it bears to other words.

The method of parsing, which the author recommends, will be seen by the following example.

Prosperity gains friends, and adversity tries them.

What part of speech is *prosperity?* Substantive. How do you know it to be a substantive? Because it can be joined to *I am thinking of.* Is it proper or common? Common. Why? Because it does not denote a particular individual. Of what number is it? Singular. Why? Because it denotes but one thing. Of what gender? It is neuter. Why? Because it is neither male nor female. To what verb does it belong? *Gains.* Is it a subject or an object? A subject.

What part of speech is *gains?* A verb. Why? Because it will take *he* before it. Is it transitive or intransitive? Transitive. Why? Because it will take *him* or *them* after it. Is it principal or auxiliary? Principal. Why? Because it represents an action. Is it finite or infinite? Finite. Why? Because it stands alone and has a subject. Why does it take the personal termination *s?* Because its subject, *prosperity*, is a substantive of the singular number. In what tense is it?

The present. Why? Because it agrees with present time. Is it used as any other part of speech? Yes. What? A substantive. Why? Because it can be joined to *I am thinking of*. How do you know it to be a verb in this sentence? Because it denotes an action.

What part of speech is *friends?* A substantive. How do you know it? Because it can be joined to *I am thinking of*. Is it proper or common? Common. Why? Because it does not denote a particular individual. Of what number is it? Plural. Why? Because it denotes more than one. Of what gender? It includes both. To what verb does it belong? To *gains*. Is it the subject or the object? The object. Is this word used as any other part of speech? No.

What part of speech is *and?* A conjunction.

Adversity and *tries* are parsed the same as *prosperity* and *gains*, except that *tries* is never used as any other part of speech.

What part of speech is *them?* A personal pronoun. Nominative or objective? Objective. What number? Plural.

PARSING TABLE.

As soon as the pupil has committed the introductory part of etymology to memory, he should be exercised in pointing out the part of speech to which each word in the following sentences belongs, also in giving the directions for distinguishing them.

SYNTACTICAL PARSING TABLE.

Article. What part of speech? Why is *a* used? Why is *an* used? Why omitted? Why repeated?

Substantive. What part of speech? How do you know it? Proper or common? Why? What number? Why? What gender? Why? To what verb or preposition does it belong? Is it the subject or the object? Is it used as any other part of speech? If it be—what? How do you know? How do you know it to be a substantive here?

Adjective. What part of speech? How do you know it? What kind? What degree? To what substantive does it belong?

Pronoun. What part of speech? What kind? Nominative or objective? What number? What person? What substantive does it stand for?

Verb. What part of speech? How do you know it? Transitive or intransitve? Why? Principal or auxiliary? Why? Finite or infinite? Why? What tense? With what time does it agree? What is its subject? Why does it take the termination—? Why does it reject the terminations? Is it used as any other part of speech? What? Why? How do you know it to be a verb here?

Participle. What part of speech? Perfect or imperfect? How is it formed? What verb is it derived from? Is it used as any other part of speech? What? Why?

Adverb. What part of speech? How do you know it?

Preposition. What part of speech? How do you know it? To what substantive or pronoun does it belong?

Conjunction. What part of speech? What is it used for?

Interjection. What part of speech?

SENTENCES TO BE PARSED.

It is the infirmity of little minds to be captivated by every appearance, and to be dazzled by every thing that sparkles.

The man who tells nothing, or who tells every thing, will equally have nothing told him.

The lips of talkers will be telling such things as appertain not unto them; but the words of such as have understanding are weighed in the balance.

The heart of fools is in their mouth, but the tongue of the wise is in his heart.

He that is truly polite knows how to contradict with respect, and to please without adulation.

The manners of a well-bred man are equally remote from insipid complaisance, and low familiarity.

A good word is an easy obligation; but not to speak ill, requires only our silence, and costs us nothing.

Wisdom is the grey hairs to a man, and unspotted life is the most venerable old age.

Let reason go before every enterprise, and counsel before every action.

Most men are friends for their own purposes, and will not abide in the day of trouble.

A friend cannot be known in prosperity; and an enemy cannot be hidden in adversity.

He who discovereth secrets loses his credit, and will never secure valuable friendships.

Honour thy father with thy whole heart, and forget not the kindness of thy mother; how canst thou recompense them the things they have done for thee?

The latter part of a wise man's life is taken up in curing the prejudices and false opinions he had contracted in the former part.

He who tells a lie is not sensible how great a task he undertakes; for he must be forced to invent twenty more to maintain it.

The prodigal robs his heir; the miser robs himself.

True wisdom consists in the regulation and government of the passions; not in a technical knowledge of arts and sciences.

Some men miss the prize of prosperity by procrastination, and others lose it by impatience and precipitancy.

He can never have a true friend who is often changing his friendships.

Beware of false reasoning when you are about to inflict an injury you cannot repair.

The finest talents would be lost in obscurity, if they were not called forth by study and cultivation.

END OF PART FIRST.

THE YOUTH'S MEMORITER.

PART THE SECOND.

VERBAL ANALYSIS.

By verbal analysis is meant the reducing of words to their elementary significations: as,

Need—less—ness, de—scribe, dem—agogue.

Words are either simple or compound: a simple or primitive word contains nothing beyond a simple element: as, *can, less, man.*

A compound or derivative word consists of two or more simple elements, producing one general signification: as,

Need—less—ness, man—ful—ness, can—not.

An element may be either a word or only part of a word: as,

Need, need—less, dem—agogue.

Elements must not be confounded with syllables.

A syllable is a combination of letters forming a simple sound, without necessarily conveying a meaning.

An element may comprise more than one syllable, and must contain a meaning, even in a separate state: as,

Can, be, less, de (from), dem (people),—a—gogue (a leader), a—cri (sharp).

The elements are for the most part derived from other languages: thus, *dem* and *agogue*, in the word *demagogue*, are derived from the Greek: *sub* and *scrib*, in the word *subscribe*, are derived from the Latin.

Elements, when derived from other languages, generally lose their original terminations: for instance, *scrib* in the original is *scribo*; hence, in rendering this word an English element, the *o* is dropped.

Elements are of three kinds: *prepositions* or *prefixes*, *terminations* or *affixes*, and *roots* or *interfixes*.

A preposition or prefix is placed at the beginning of a word: as,

Merit, *de*merit; legal, *il*legal.

A termination, or affix, usually changes a word from one part of speech to another: as,

Love, lov*ing*, love*ly*, love*liness*.

Prepositions and terminations may be joined either to simple or compound words: as,

*Amphi*theatre; moveable, *im*moveable.

A root, or interfix, is an element which constitutes the basis or essential part of a word: as,

*Art*ful, *assist*ant.

Roots are frequently combined with one another: as,

*Lord*ship, *demagogue*.

In compounding, the letters of the elements are sometimes changed: as,

Long, length, extend, extensive.

Letters are also frequently dropped: as,

Trans when compounded with *spire*, drops the final *s*, *transpire* not *transspire*.

For the sake of euphony, letters are sometimes added: as,

Re when compounded with *und*, re—*d*—undant.

The following examples will shew the manner in which the elements are derived and combined.

Acri, aci, acu, are derived from the Latin words *acris,* sharp, and *acuo, to make sharp;* hence we have *acrid, acid, acute.*

Scrib and *scrip* are derived from *scribo,* to write, and *scriptum,* written; from which we form the following words:

    ble, *to do* .... scri*ble*
    sub, *under* .... *sub*scribe
    in, *within* .... *in*scribe
    post, *after* .... *post*script
    de, *from* .... *de*scribe
    circum, *around* .... *circum*scribe

and many others.

Scop is derived from the Greek word *skopeo, to view,* or *see,* from which we have the following words:

    tele, *distant* .... *tele*scope
    anemo, *the wind* .... *anemo*scope
    micro, *small* .... *micro*scope
    horo, *an hour* .... *horo*scope

As experience tells us that we cannot see the wind, it will readily occur to the mind that *anemoscope* is an instrument to show the direction in which the wind blows.

PREPOSITIONS OR PREFIXES.

PREPOSITIONS FROM THE GREEK.

Prepositions and meanings.	Examples.
amphi, *both*	*amph*ibious
amphi, *round, about*	*amph*itheatre
ana, *again*	*ana*baptist
anti, *against, opposed to*	*anti*christian
ant, ——	*ant*arctic
apo, *from*	*apo*stle
ap, ——	*ap*helion
a, *not*	*a*theist
cata, *down, against, according to*	*cata*logue
cate, ——	*cate*chise
dis, *two, to separate, to undo a thing, from*	*dis*arm
di, ——	*di*verge, *di*vest
dia, *through*	*dia*meter
epi, *upon, over*	*epi*taph, *epi*scopal
ep, ——	*ep*hemera
hypo, *under*	*hypo*crite
hyper, *beyond*	*hyper*critic
meta, *between*	*meta*chronism

VERBAL ANALYSIS.

Prepositions and meanings.	Examples.
meta, *to carry*	*meta*phor
——— *again*	*meta*morphosis
para, *through*	*para*graph
——— *with*	*para*phrase
——— *contrary to*	*para*dox
——— *by the side of*	*para*clete
peri, *round, about*	*peri*cranium
semi, *half*	*semi*circle
demi, ———	*demi*god
hemi, ———	*hemi*sphere
sym, *with, together*	*sym*pathy
syn, ———	*syn*onymy
syl, ———	*syl*lable
sys, ———	*sys*tem

PREPOSITIONS FROM THE LATIN.

a, *away, from, on, to, not, in, without*	*a*side
ab, ———	*ab*use
abs, ———	*abs*olve
ad, *to, at, together*	*ad*join
ac, ———	*ac*count
af, ———	*af*fair
al, ———	*al*lay
ag, ———	*ag*grieve
ap, ———	*ap*point
as, ———	*as*sent
ante, *before*	*ante*chamber

Prepositions and meanings.	Examples.
circum, *around*	*circum*scribe
con, *with, together*	*con*join
com, —	*com*motion
co, —	*co*equal
col, —	*col*lateral
cor, —	*cor*relative
cog, —	*cog*nate
contra, *against*	*contra*dict
counter, —	*counter*act
de, *down, from*	*de*base
— *to undo*	*de*face
— *wanting*	*de*merit
e, *out of*	*e*migrate
ec, —	*ec*centric
ef, —	*ef*face
ex, —	*ex*change
in, *in, into, on, not*	*in*lay
ig, —	*ig*noble
il, —	*il*legal
im, —	*im*print
ir, —	*ir*reparable
inter, *among*	*inter*view
— *between*	*inter*line
intro, *within*	*intro*duce
ob, *to, from, opposed to, against*	*ob*struct
op, —	*op*pose
oc, —	*oc*cident
per, *through*	*per*form
— *thoroughly*	*per*fect

Prepositions and meanings.	Examples.
pre, *before*	*pre*fix
post, *after*	*post*cript
pro, *forth*	*pro*duce
—— *forward*	*pro*vident
—— *before*	*pro*chronism
—— *for*	*pro*consul
preter, *beyond*	*preter*natural
re, *again, back*	*re*turn
se, *apart*	*se*lect
— *without*	*se*cure
sine, *without*	*sine*cure
sub, *under*	*sub*scribe
sup, —	*sup*plant
suc, —	*suc*cess
suf, —	*suf*focate
sug, —	*sug*gest
sus, —	*sus*tain
super, *above*	*super*scription
—— *over*	*super*abound
subter, *under*	*subter*fuge
trans, *beyond*	*trans*port
tra, ——	*tra*duce
ultra, *beyond*	*ultra*marine

PREPOSITIONS FROM THE SAXON.

after, *behind*	*after*noon
be, *about, for*	*be*sprinkle
— *before*	*be*speak
en, *to make*	*en*noble

Prepositions and meanings.	Examples.
em, *in*	*em*bryo
for, *not*	*for*bid
fore, *before*	*fore*see
gain, *against*	*gain*say
hind, *behind*	*hind*most
mis, *wrong*	*mis*pell
—— *against*	*mis*belief
over, *superiority*	*over*come
—— *to alter*	*over*throw
out, *superiority*	*out*run
—— *beyond*	*out*ward
un, *not*	*un*worthy
— *to undo*	*un*fold
up, *upwards*	*up*hold
— *to overthrow*	*up*set
under, *below*	*under*go
—— *defect*	*under*value

TERMINATIONS OR AFFIXES.

VERBS.

Affixes and significations.	Examples.
en, *to make*	heigh*ten*
ate, *to make, to do*	crimin*ate*
ize, *to make*	equal*ize*
ise —	chast*ise*
ify —	beaut*ify*
fy, —	justi*fy*

VERBAL ANALYSIS.

Affixes and significations.	Examples.
ble, *to do*	scri*ble*

ADJECTIVES.

ant,	*being a, or an,*	attend*ant*
ent,	—	consist*ent*
ous,	*having*	covet*ous*
an,	*of or belonging to*	Europe*an*
ine,	—	serpent*ine*
ar,	—	angul*ar*
ary	—	custom*ary*
ory,	—	contradict*ory*
ic,	—	angel*ic*
al,	—	brut*al*
ical,	—	method*ical*
ive,	*that can do*	extens*ive*
able,	*that can be, or is worthy to bear, suffer, or receive*	admiss*able*
ible,	—	access*ible*
ile,	—	project*ile*
ful,	*abounding*	art*ful*
some,	*somewhat*	trouble*some*
most,	*extreme*	out*most*
ward,	*in the direction of*	back*ward*
ly,	*like*	beggar*ly*
y,	*plenty*	wealth*y*
ish,	*of the substansive*	Engl*ish*
en,	*of, composed of*	wood*en*
less,	*not*	need*less*

SUBSTANTIVES DENOTING THE PERSON.

ar,	*he or she is a or an*	schol*ar*
er,	——	farm*er*
or,	——	debt*or*
ary,	——	mission*ary*
eer,	——	auction*eer*
ee,	——	debauch*ee*
an,	*he or she is of or belonging to*	christi*an*
ist,	——	calvin*ist*
ite,	——	fox*ite*
ant,	*one who does or is*	assist*ant*
ent,	——	confid*ent*
ster,	——	mal*ster*
ard,	*nature, disposition*	slugg*ard*

SUBSTANTIVES DENOTING THE THING.

ment,	*the thing done, or the state of a thing*	abate*ment*
mony,	——	patri*mony*
ity,	——	absur*dity*
ty	——	royal*ty*
y,	——	eupho*ny*
age,	——	broker*age*
ation,	——	defam*ation*
ition,	——	defin*ition*
tion,	——	consump*tion*
ion,	——	apprehens*ion*
ice,	——	serv*ice*

VERBAL ANALYSIS.

ance, *the thing done, or the state of a thing* .... abund*ance*
ence, ——— .... confid*ence*
ancy, ——— .... const*ancy*
ency, ——— .... tend*ency*
tude, ——— .... longi*tude*
cy, *office,* .... magistra*cy*
head, — .... God*head*
ary, *place* .... grana*ry*
ory, — .... observato*ry*
ery, — .... brew*ery*
s, *added to* ic *converts the adjective into a substantive* . optic*s*
ure, *the thing produced* .... creat*ure*
ism, *profession* .... bapt*ism*
hood, *state of a person* ...... knight*hood*
ship, *office or state* .... lord*ship*
ness, *from the quality* .... black*ness*
dom, *place, country, or state* king*dom*
t, *a contraction of the participle* joint *from* joined
th, *from the adjective and verb* leng*th*
ing, *the imperfect participle used as a substantive* . a see*ing*
er, *belonging to* .... pray*er*
by, ——— .... brave*ry*
acy, ——— .... accur*acy*

ADVERBS.

ly, *like* .... shameful*ly*
ward, *in the direction of* .... to*ward*

wise, *manner* .... like*wise*
ways, ... straight*ways*

St, at the beginning of a word, denotes strength and stability: as,

*S*trength, *s*tability, *s*tay, *s*taff, *s*tate, *s*tout, &c.

Str expresses violence and energy: as,

*Str*ike, *str*etch, *str*ive, &c.

Thr, rapidity or force: as,

*Thr*ob, *thr*ough, *thr*ow, *thr*ust, &c.

Wr, bending or turning out of the way: as,

*Wr*eck, *wr*ap, *wr*y, *wr*ing, *wr*ath, *wr*ong, &c.

Sw, motion sideways or sliding: as,

*Sw*ing, *sw*ay, *sw*erve, *sw*im, &c.

Sl, gently falling: as,

*Sl*ide, *sl*ing, *sl*ip, *sl*y, *sl*it, &c.

Sp, spreading and wasting: as,

*Sp*it, *sp*read, *sp*rinkle, *sp*ill, &c.

Ash, at the end of a word, denotes quickness or sharpness: as,

Cr*ash*, fl*ash*, l*ash*, g*ash*, &c.

Ush denotes a blunt sort of motion: as,

Cr*ush*, h*ush*, br*ush*, &c.

Ose is an augmentative affix and signifies *full*: as,

Verb*ose*, *full of words*.

Ule, cle, and *cul,* are diminutives and signify *little*: as,

Animal*cule, a little animal;* corpus*cle, a small body;* denti*cul*ated, *set with small teeth.*

ROOTS OR INTERFIXES.

ROOTS FROM THE GREEK.

[In words and roots derived from the Greek, *ch* is sounded like *k*, and *ph* like *f*. When incombinable consonants come together, the first must not be sounded: thus, *digm* is pronounced *dim*; *pneu* is pronounced *neu*. When, however, two incombinable consonants fall in the middle of a word, and can be separated, they must both be pronounced: as, *mn* in *amnesty*.]

Roots and meanings.	Examples.
acro, *the top, the extremity*	acrostic *
aer, *the air*	aerology
acou, *sound, hearing*	acoustics
ace, *cure*	panacea
adelphia, *a brother*	monadelphia
æres, *to cut*	diæresis
agogue, *a leader*	demagogue
agon, *strife*	agonistes
algi, *pain*	cephalgi
ali, —	cephalic
alecto, *a cock,*	alectoromachy †
alle, *another*	parallel
antho, *a flower*	anthology
anthrop, *a man*	misanthrope ‡

* A poem in which the initials form a name.   † A cock fight.
‡ *Mis*, against, and *anthrop*, a man—a hater of mankind.

Roots and meanings.	Examples.
anemo, *the wind*	*anemo*scope
arch, *chief, government*	mon*arch*
arith, *numbers*	*arith*metic
aræ, *thin*	*aræ*ometer *
arist, *greatest, noblest*	*arist*ocracy
astro, *a star*	*astro*nomy
ascet, *fervent*	*ascet*ic
atmo, *vapour*	*atmo*sphere
auto, *by one's self*	*auto*crat
auli, *a pipe*	hydr*auli*c
axio, *worthy, evident*	*axio*m
bas, *a foot, low*	*bas*e †
bapti, *to dip,*	*bapti*ze
baro, *weight*	*baro*meter
bio, *life*	amphi*bio*us
bite, —	ceno*bite*s
bibl, *a book*	*bibl*ical
bront, *thunder*	*bront*ology
broncho, *the throat*	*broncho*tomy
bros, *mortal*	am*bros*ia ‡
bryo, *to grow*	em*bryo*
brachy, *short*	*brachy*graphy
buco, *an ox*	*buco*lic

* An instrument for measuring thin fluids.

† *Bass,* the lowest notes in music, a mat for the feet.—*base,* low, mean, the lowest part of a building, &c.—*Bassoon,* an instrument on which low tones are produced.—*Bask,* to lie on the ground, &c.

‡ Am*bros*ia, food of the gods.

VERBAL ANALYSIS.

Roots and meanings.	Examples.
byss, *the bottom*	a*byss*
catholi, *universal*	*catholi*c
caus, *to burn*	*caus*tic
caut, ——	*caut*erise
cac, *bad*	*cac*oethes
cele, *a swelling*	hydro*cele*
ceph, *the head*	*ceph*alic
ceme, *sleep*	*ceme*tery*
ceno, *empty,*	*ceno*taph
——, *common*	*ceno*bites
chron, *time*	*chron*ology
chao, *confusion*	*chao*tic
—— *air*	*chao*mancy
chris, *to anoint,*	*Chris*t
choro, *a region*	*choro*graphy
chy, *juice*	*chy*le
chrom, *colour*	*chrom*atic
chiro, *a hand*	*chiro*graphy
chyny, *a habit*	caco*chyny*
chili, *a thousand*	*chili*st †
chol, *bile*	*chol*er
clima, *a ladder*	*clima*te
clete, *to call*	para*clete* ‡
cosm, *the world*	micro*cosm*
comb, *hollow*	cata*comb*
comi, *praise*	en*comi*um
chryst, *ice, (clear)*	*chryst*al

* A burial place. † One who believes that Christ will reign a thousand years upon earth. ‡ The Holy Ghost.

Roots and meanings.	Examples.
cryp, *hidden*	*cryp*tic
crani, *the skull*	peri*crani*um
crit, *to judge*	*crit*ic
cris, ——	hypo*cris*y
crat, *to rule*	auto*crat*
cracy, ——	demo*cracy*
cycl, *a circle*	*cycl*opœdia
cynic, *to snarl*	*cynic*al
dactyl, *a finger, a ring*	*dactyl*e *
dæmon, *a devil*	pan*dæmon*ium †
demon, ——	*demon*iac
dem, *the people*	*dem*agogue
deca, *ten*	*deca*gon
deuter, *second*	*deuter*onomy ‡
derm, *the skin*	epi*derm*is
didac, *teaching*	*didac*tic
diplo, *to treat with*	*diplo*matic
——, *to confer*	*diplo*ma
didym, *twins*	*didym*oitocia
digm, *to shew*	para*digm*
dox, *opinion*	ortho*dox*
—— *glory*	*dox*ology
—— *to seem*	para*dox*
dodeca, *twelve*	*dodeca*gon
drom, *a course*	hippo*drom*
dynam, *power*	*dynam*ics
dys, *bad*	*dys*pepsia

* A poetic foot. † *Pan*, all, i. e. all devils—Hell. ‡ The second book of the law.

VERBAL ANALYSIS.

Roots and meanings.	Examples.
ecclesia, *the church*	ecclesiastic
ecdote, *published*	anecdote *
echi, *to sound*	catechise
echo, —	echoing
edro, *a base*	icosaedron
egyri, *(to praise,) to collect*	panegyric
eido, *a form*	eidouranion
elas, *to repel*	elastic
elee, *alms, pity*	eleemosynary
almo, —	almoner
ennea, *nine*	enneagon
endec, *eleven*	endecagon
ero, *love*	erotic
erg, *a work*	energy
ether, *air*	ethereal
ethis, *a custom*	cacoethis
eudio, *purity of air*	eudiometer
ev, *good*	evangelist †
eu, —	eulogy
exy, *habit*	cachexy
fant, *an appearance*	fantasy
gam, *marriage*	misogamist
galax, *milk*	galaxy ‡
gast, *the stomach*	gastric
geo, *the earth*	geology
genethli, *a generation*	genethliacal
glossa, *a tongue*	glossary

* A, not, changed to *an.* † Ev*angel*ist is derived from *angel*, a messenger. ‡ The milky way.

VERBAL ANALYSIS.

Roots and meanings.   **Examples.**

Root	Example
glot, *a tongue*	poly*glot*
gni, *to know*	co*gni*tion
gno, ———	pro*gno*sticate
gon, *an angle*	deca*gon*
gor, *to speak*	cate*gor*y
gram, *a letter*	*gram*mar
——— *a writing*	pro*gram*ma
——— *a figure*	dia*gram*
graph, *to write*	penta*graph*
——— *to describe*	geo*graph*y
glyph, *to carve*	hiero*glyph*ic
griph, *a net*	logo*griph* *
gymn, *strong exercise, naked*	*gymn*astics
gyni, *a woman*	miso*gyn*ist
helio, *the sun*	*helio*centric
hetro, *another, unlike*	*hetro*genus
hedri, *a seat*	san*hedrim* †
hepta, *seven*	*hepta*gon
hexa, *six*	*hexa*gon
hendec, *eleven*	*hendec*agon
hemer, *a day*	ep*hemer*is
hæmo, *blood*	*hæmo*rrhage
horizo, *to limit*	*horizo*ntal
hebdoma, *a week*	*hebdoma*dal
hecato, *a hundred*	*hecato*mb ‡
hier, *sacred*	*hier*archy
hippo, *a horse*	*hippo*drom

* A word in a net—a riddle. † The supreme counsel of the Jews. ‡ A sacrifice of a hundred oxen.

Roots and meanings.	Examples.
homo, *like, the same*	*homo*geny
hygr, *moisture*	*hygr*ometer
hydr, *water*	*hydr*aulics
ichno, *a mark*	*ichno*graphy *
icon, *a picture or image*	*icon*ology
icosa, *twenty*	*icosa*edron
ichthy, *a fish*	*ichthy*ology
idio, *peculiar*	*idio*m
iso, *equal,*	*iso*sceles
lab, *to take*	syl*lab*us
leth, *forgetfulness*	*leth*argy
lexico, *a dictionary*	*lexico*grapher
lemma, *an argument*	di*lemma*
litho, *a stone*	*litho*graphy
log, *a word or discourse*	aero*log*y
lys, *to dissolve*	ana*lys*is
lyt, ——	ana*lyt*ic
mach, *a fight*	nau*mach*y
mani, *madness*	*mani*ac
math, *instruction, learning*	*math*ematics
martyr, *a witness*	*martyr*ology
mano, *thin*	*mano*meter †
macro, *large*	*macro*cosm
mazo, *a breast*	a*mazo*n ‡

* A ground plot.

† An instrument for ascertaining the density of air.

‡ The Amazonians were an athletic race of women, who are said to have cut off their breasts to make themselves resemble men.

VERBAL ANALYSIS.

Roots and meanings.	Examples.
mancy, *divination or magic*	geo*mancy*
mega, *great*	*mega*cosm
melan, *black*	*melan*choly
mel, *honey or sweetness*	oxy*mel*
metro, *a mother*	*metro*polis
met, *to measure*	arith*met*ic
micro, *little*	*micro*scope
miso, *to hate*	*miso*gamist
mim, *to mimic*	panto*mim*e
mnes, *to remember*	a*mnes*ty
morphos, *a form*	meta*morphos*e
mon, *one, alone*	*mon*arch
mytho, *a fable*	*mytho*logy
my, *to wink*	*my*opes
neo, *new*	*neo*pyhte
necro, *dead*	*necro*mancy
nom, *a rule*	eco*nom*y
noma, —	a*noma*ly
nona, *nine*	*nona*gon
oblivi, *forgetfulness*	*oblivi*on
ocra, *power, rule*	aut*ocra*t
oct, *eight*	*oct*agon
ochlo, *the multitude*	*ochlo*cracy
ochi, *to dwell, a dwelling-place*	par*ochi*al
oec, ————	ant*oec*i
eco, ————	*eco*nomy
ode, *a song*	epis*ode*
ody, —	mel*ody*
edy, —	com*edy*

VERBAL ANALYSIS.

Roots and meanings.	Examples.
odu, *a way*	Ex*odu*s *
odyn, *pain*	an*odyn*e
odo, *a tooth*	*odo*ntic
olig, *few*	*olig*archy
ono, *a name or word*	*ono*matopœia
ony, ——	met*ony*my
any, ——	par*any*mous
onto, *a being*	*onto*logy
opsi, *late*	*opsi*mathy
ops, *a view*	syn*ops*is
ophthalm, *the eye*	*ophthalm*ic
opt, ——	*opt*ic
oply, *armour*	pan*oply*
orcis, *to adjure*	ex*orcis*e
ortho, *correct*	*ortho*graphy
ornitho, *a bird*	*ornitho*logy
oris, *to define*	aph*oris*m
orgi, *a work*	ge*orgi*c
orama, *a view*	pan*orama*
oste, *a bone*	peri*oste*um
† ostra, *censure*	*ostra*cism
ota, *the ear*	*ot*algia
oxy, *acid*	*oxy*gen
—— *sharp*	par*oxy*sm

* The book of Exodus details the events that occurred while the children of Israel were on their *way* to the land of promise.

† Literally signifies an oyster-shell. The Athenians, when they passed a public censure, wrote upon oyster-shells and cast them into an urn.

VERBAL ANALYSIS.

Roots and meanings.	Examples.
path, *feeling*	a*path*y
pæia, *to make*	pharmaco*pœia*
pœia, ——	prosopo*pœia*
pan, *all*	*pan*acea
panto, ——	*panto*mime
pædia, *instruction*	cyclo*pædia*
pason, *all*	dia*pason* *
palin, *again*	*palin*drome
pate, *to walk*	peri*patetic* †
ped, *a boy*	*ped*agogue
pod, *a foot*	tri*pod*
pus, ——	poly*pus*
penta, *five*	*penta*gonal
peps, *digestion*,	dis*peps*ia
penteco, *fifty*	*penteco*st ‡
penthe, *pain*	ne*penthe*
phag, *to eat or consume*	anthropo*phagi*,
phon, *sound or speech*	sym*phony*
phtho, *sound*	di*phtho*ng
philo, *love*	*philo*math
phil, ——	*phil*anthropy
phan, *a shadow*	*phan*tom
phobia, *dread*	hydro*phobia* ‖
physi, *nature*	*physi*cs

* A chord in music which includes all the tones.
† Philosophers who used to discourse while walking about.
‡ A fifty days' feast among the Jews.
‖ Canine madness, so called because one of the symptoms is a dread of water.

VERBAL ANALYSIS.

Roots and meanings.   **Examples.**

phragm, *a fence*	dia*phragm*
phyte, *to grow*	neo*phyte*
—— *a plant*	zoo*phite*
pherna, *a dower*	para*phernalia*
pher, *to carry*	peri*phery*
phor, ——	phos*phorus*
phrase, *a speech*	para*phrase*
phos, *light*	*phos*phorus
phe, *to speak*	pro*phet*
pharm, *medicine*	*pharm*acy
plan, *to wander*	*plan*et
plex, *to strike*	apo*plex*y
pneuma, *air, spirits*	*pneuma*tics
pnœa, *to breathe*	dys*pnœa*
poly, *many*	*poly*gon
pothegm, *to say*	apo*thegm*
polis, *a city*	metro*polis*
pol, *to sell*	mono*poly*
polem, *war*	*polem*ics
potamus, *a river*	hippo*potamus*
proto, *the first*	*proto*martyr
pragma, *business*	*pragma*tic
prosopo, *a person*	*prosopo*pœia
pseudo, *false*	*pseudo*prophet
psych, *the soul*	*psych*omachy
pyro, *fire*	*pyro*techny
pylac, *to defend*	pro*pylac*tics
rac, *to dash*	cata*rac*t
rhap, *to sow at random*	*rhap*sody

VERBAL ANALYSIS.

rhetor, *a speaker*	......	*rhetor*ic
rheu, *to flow*	....	*rheu*m
rrh, ——	....	cata*rrh*
rhym, *a rule*	....	*rhym*e
rhythm, ——	....	*rhythm*
sarco, *flesh*	....	*sarco*phagus
sbestos, *to burn*	......	a*sbestos* *
sceles, *a leg*	....	iso*sceles*
sci, *a shadow*	....	amphi*sci*a
scop, *to view*	....	tele*scop*e
sep, *to putrefy*	......	anti*sep*tic
site, (*to flatter,*)*corn,*	..	para*site* †
soph, *wisdom*	....	philo*soph*ic
—— *deception*	......	*soph*ist
sphere, *a ball*	....	hemi*sphere*
stle, *to send*	....	apo*stle*
stic, *a line or verse*	....	acro*stic*
steno, *short*	....	*steno*graphy
static, *to weigh*	......	hydro*static*
stentor, *loud*	....	*stentor*ian
stroph, *to turn*	......	cata*stroph*y
stere, *solid*	....	*stere*otype
sylu, *to pillage*	......	a*sylu*m
taph, *a tomb*	......	epi*taph*
techni, *art or science*	....	*techni*cal
techny ——	....	poly*techny*
tetra, *four*	....	*tetra*gon

* A fossil, which, when made into cloth, forms a garment which resists the power of fire.

† One who earns his bread by flattering the wealthy.

Roots and meanings.	Examples.
tele, *distant*	*tele*graph
teuch, *a book*	penta*teuch*
the, *God*	*the*ology
— *topic*	*the*me *
thalam, *marriage*	epi*thalam*ium
thana, *death*	eu*thana*sia
theca, *a repository*	biblio*theca*
tome, *a book*	*tome*
tocia, *to bring forth*	didymoi*tocia*
tom, *to cut*	ana*tom*y
— —	epi*tome*
ton, *a tone*	*ton*ic
topo, *a place*	*topo*graphy
tri, *three*	*tri*pod
† uran, *heaven*	*Urania* ‡
zeal, *to be hot*	*zeal*ous
zone, zod, *a girdle*	*zod*iac
zoo, *an animal*	*zoo*logy

ROOTS FROM THE LATIN.

acri, *sharp, sour*	*acri*d
aci, ——	*aci*d
acu, ——	*acu*te
acet, ——	*acet*ate
act, *acting*	*act*ion

* A subject proposed. † By dropping the initial or first letter. ‡ The goddess of astronomy.

K

Roots and meanings.	Examples.
agi, *acting*	ag*i*tate
dig, ——	prod*ig*al
git, ——	cog*it*ate
agu, ——	coa*gu*late *
adipo, *fat*	*adip*ous
adula, *to flatter*	*adula*tion
æstu, estu, *the tide*	*estu*ary
agra, *fields*	*agra*rian
agri, ——	*agri*culture
algi, *cold*	*algi*d
ali, *to nourish*	*ali*ment
—— *another*	*ali*en
alt, *lofty*	*alt*itude
alter, *another*	*alter*nate
ulter, ——	ad*ulter*ate
ala, *a wing*	*ala*crity
ale, ——	*ale*rt
albu, *white*	*albu*gineous
ama, *love, friendship,*	*ama*tory
ami, ——	*ami*cable
amo, ——	*amo*rous
imi, *love, friendship*	in*imi*cal
ambul, *to walk*	*ambul*ate
ambi, *to surround*	*ambi*ent
ampl, *large*	*ampl*ify
angu, *a corner*	*angu*lar
ang, ——	*ang*le
anim, *mind,*	*anim*ate

* The acting together of substances so as to produce curd.

VERBAL ANALYSIS.

Roots and meanings.	Examples.
anim, *soul*	magn*anim*ity
—— *violence*	*anim*osity
annu, *a circle*	*annu*lar
—— *a year*	*annu*al
enni, ——	per*enni*al
aperi, *to open*	*aperi*ent
api, *a bee*	*api*ary
aqua, *water*	*aqua*tic
aque, ——	*aque*ous
arch, *a bow*	*arch*ery
arbit, *to judge*	*arbit*rate
arbor, *a tree*	*arbor*escent
ard, *heat*	*ard*our
ara, *to plough*	*ara*ble
ardu, *steep*	*ardu*ous
asper, *rough, sharp*	*asper*ity
ascerv, *a heap*	co*ascerv*ate
atro, *base, wicked*	*atro*city
audi, *to hear*	*audi*ence
auri, ——	*auri*cular
—— *gold*	*auri*graphy
auc, *to increase*	*auc*tion *
aut, ——	*aut*hor
aug, ——	*aug*ment
—— *great*	*aug*ust
auspi, *protection, favour*	*auspi*cious †
auda, *bold*	*auda*cious

* To increase the price at each bidding. † This root is derived from a compound of *avis*, a bird, and *specio*, to look.

Roots and meanings.	Examples.
auxili, *aid*	*auxili*ary
avi, *a bird*	*avi*ary
ava, *to covet*	*ava*rice
avid, ——	*avid*ity
barb, *a beard*	*barb*er
bel, *war*	re*bel*
bell, ——	*bell*igerent
—— *fair*	em*bell*ish
bene, *well, kind*	*bene*ficent
beni, ——	*beni*gn
beati, *blessed*	*beati*fy
bi, *twice, two, twofold*	*bi*ennial
bis, ——	*bis*sect
bin, ——	com*bin*e
bib, *to drink*	im*bib*e
bon, *good*	*bon*ny
brue, *to soak,*	im*brue*
bue, *to tincture*	im*bue*
brev, *short*	*brev*ity
brum, *winter*	*brum*al
bulb, *a round root*	*bulb*ous
bust, *burnt*	com*bust*
calor, *heat*	*calor*ic
cant, *to sing*	re*cant*
cent, ——	ac*cent*
cis, *to cut, fall, or kill*	de*cis*ion
cid, ——	pari*cid*e
sec, ——	*sec*tion
cad, *to fall*	*cad*ence

VERBAL ANALYSIS.

Roots and meanings.	Examples.
cay, *to fall*	de*cay*
cas, —	*cas*cade
cap, *to take*	*cap*ture
cep, —	ex*cep*t
cip, —	anti*cip*ate
cup, —	oc*cup*y
ceiv, —	con*ceiv*e
ceip, —	re*ceip*t
caut, *to avoid*	*caut*ion
cav, ——	*cav*eat
— *hollow*	*cav*e
cani, *a dog*	*cani*ne
cand, *white, fair*	*cand*id
— *to shine*	*cand*le
castig, *to punish*	*castig*ate
catena, *a chain*	con*catena*tion
carcer, *a prison*	in*carcer*ate
calig, *darkness*	*calig*inous
carn, *flesh*	*carn*al
ca, —	*ca*daverous *
carbon, *coal*	*carbon*ize
cede, *to go, to depart*	inter*cede*
ceed, ——	pro*ceed*
cess, ——	pro*cess*
ceas, ——	de*cease*
celer, *quick*	*celer*ity
censu, *to judge*	*censu*re

* *Ca*, flesh—*da*, given—*ver*, worm—flesh given to worms: hence cadaverous means a dead body.

Roots and meanings.	Examples.
cern, *to distinguish*	dis*cern*
cert, *sure, certain*	as*cert*ain
cell, *a cavity*	*cell*ar
centr, *the centre*	ex*centr*ic
cent, *a hundred*	*cent*uary
celib, *a bachelor*	*celib*acy
ceal, *to hide*	con*ceal*
ceci, *blind*	*ceci*ty
celes, *heaven*	*celes*tial
cera, *wax*	*cera*te
cere, ——	*cere*ment *
chart, *paper*	*chart*er
cicatr, *a scar*	*cicatr*ize
cite, *to call, to move*	ex*cite*
cita, ——	*cita*tion
cili, ——	con*cili*ate
cile, ——	recon*cile*
civi, *a citizen*	*civi*lize
cinct, *to bind*	suc*cinct* †
cipi, *to begin*	in*cipi*ent
clam, *loud*	*clam*orous
claim, ——	de*claim*
clud, *to shut*	ex*clud*e
clos, ——	*clos*e
clin, *to bend*	in*clin*e
clen, ——	de*clen*sion
cliv, ——	ac*cliv*ity

* A waxed cloth, in which dead bodies are wrapped.
† Bound up; hence short, concise.

Roots and meanings.	Examples.
clemen, *mild*	*clemen*cy
coc, *to boil*	de*coc*tion
copi, *plenty*	*copi*ous
cord, *heart*	con*cord*
corp, *a body*	*corp*ulent
cour, *to run*	*cour*se
cur, —	*cur*rent
commod, *to profit*	ac*commod*ate
cola, *to strain*	*cola*nder
cost, *side*	ac*cost* *
coron, *a crown*	*coron*ation
cortica, *bark of a tree*	de*cortica*te
cornu, *a horn*	*cornu*copia
corni, —	*corni*cle
corn, —	uni*corn*
corusca, *glittering*	*corusca*tion
coloss, *enormous*	*coloss*ean
cred, *belief*	*cred*ence
creed, —	*creed*
cret, *to grow or increase*	con*cret*e
cru, —	ac*cru*e
— *cruel*	*cruel*ty
cras, *to-morrow*	pro*cras*tinate
crema, *to burn*	*crema*tion
cruci, *a cross*	*cruci*fix
cult, *to till*	*cult*ivate
colo, —	*colo*ny
cub, *to sit on*	in*cub*ation

* Bending sides together or at the same time.

Roots and meanings.	Examples.
cumb, *to bend or lie down*	re*cumb*ent
curi, *care*	*curi*ous
cura, —	*cura*te
cure, —	se*cure*
culp, *a fault*	*culp*able
cus, *to shake*	dis*cus*s
— *to strike*	ac*cus*e
cumul, *a heap*	ac*cumul*ate
culmin, *the top*	*culmin*ate
custo, *guard*	*custo*dy
culin, *a kitchen*	*culin*ary
cuta, *the skin*	*cuta*neous
curt, *to shorten*	*curt*ail
damn, *to hurt*	*damn*ify
demn, —	in*demn*ity
dei, *God*	*dei*ty
div, —	*div*ine
deem, *to buy*	re*deem*
demp, —	re*demp*tion
dense, *thick*	con*dense*
dent, *a tooth*	*dent*ist
dexter, *right, expert*	*dexter*ity
deli, *to blot out*	in*deli*ble
decor, *graceful*	*decor*ous
—— *ornamental*	*decor*ate
dict, *to speak*	contra*dict*
digni, *worthy*	*digni*ty
diurn, *a day*	*diurn*al
dia, —	meri*dia*n

VERBAL ANALYSIS.

Roots and meanings.	Examples.
diabo, *the devil*	*diabo*lical
domin, *a lord*	*domin*ion
dona, *to give*	*dona*tion
da, —	ca*da*verous
dit, —	ad*dit*ion
dat, —	*dat*ive
dote, —	anti*dote*
do, —	en*do*w
dors, *the back*	en*dors*e
dom, *a house*	*dom*estic
doc, *to learn*	*doc*ile
— *learned*	*doc*tor
dole, *to grieve*	con*dole*
dorm, *to sleep*	*dorm*ant
dura, *hard*	*dura*ble
duc, *to lead*	intro*duc*e
dubi, *to doubt*	in*dubi*table
dulc, *sweet*	*dulc*et
du, *two*	*du*et
— *to put on*	en*du*e
ebri, *drunk*	in*ebri*ety
edi, *a building*	*edi*fice
— *to eat*	*edi*ble
ego, *I*	*ego*tism
equi, *equal*	*equi*distant
equa, —	ad*equa*te
eque, *a horse*	*eque*rry
err, *to wander*	*err*atic

Roots and meanings.	Examples.
ert, *active*	in*ert* *
— *to bear*	ex*ert*
erc, *to force*	co*erce* †
este, *to value*	*este*em
esti, ——	*esti*mate
ess, *to be*	*ess*ence
ent, ——	non*ent*ity
escu, *food*	*escu*lent
eva, *a time*	co*eva*l
exigu, *thin*	*exigu*ous
fatu, *foolish*	*fatu*ity
fac, *to do or make*	manu*fac*ture
fit, ——	bene*fit*
fic, ——	bene*fice*
fec, ——	af*fec*t
far, *corn or flour*	*far*inaceous
fabul, *to converse*	con*fabul*ate
falla, *to deceive, to err*	*falla*cious
falli, ——	in*falli*ble
fabr, *a workman*	*fabr*ic
fastid, *pride*	*fastid*ious
faceti, *merry*	*faceti*ous
fess, *to acknowledge*	con*fess*
fer, *to carry*	con*fer*
— *to boil*	*fer*vent
ferru, *iron*	*ferru*ginous
fen, *to force*	de*fen*d

From *fero*, by cutting off the initial. † From *arceo*, by changing the initial.

VERBAL ANALYSIS.

Roots and meanings.	Examples.
fecu, *dregs*	*fecu*lent
— *fruitful*	*fecu*ndity
feli, *happy*	*feli*city
fem, *a woman*	*fem*inine
feroc, *savage*	*feroc*ity
fede, *an agreement*	*fede*ral
feti, *foul*	*feti*d
femor, *the thigh*	*femor*al
fila, *a thread*	*fila*ment
fide, *faith*	con*fide*nt
fix, *to place*	cruci*fix*
fic, *to form*	*fic*tion
fig, *to make*	*fig*ure
fin, *the end*	*fin*ite
fisca, *money*,	con*fisca*te
fili, *son or daughter*	*fili*al
fia, *let it be done*	*fia*t
fiss, *to split*	*fiss*ure
flex, *to bend*	*flex*ible
flec, ———	re*flec*t
fluct, *a wave*	*fluct*uate
flict, *to smite*	af*flict*
flu, *to flow*	*flu*ent
flux, ———	re*flux*
flat, *wind*	in*flat*e
flagr, *to burn*	con*flagr*ation
flam, *a flame*	in*flam*mable
foli, *a leaf*	ex*foli*ate
foca, *a chimney*	suf*foca*te *

* Literally, under a chimney; figuratively, to choke.

Roots and meanings.	Examples.
form, *a shape*	*form*ation
formid, *to fear*	*formid*able
for, *to bore*	per*for*ate
fortu, *chance*	*fortu*itous
frac, *to break*	*frac*ture
fringe, ——	in*fringe*
frag, ——	*frag*ment
frang, ——	*frang*ible
frai, ——	*frai*l
frater, *a brother*	*frater*nal
fratr, ——	*fratr*icide
fragr, *to smell sweet*	*fragr*ant
fric, *to rub*	*fric*tion
frain, *a bridle*	re*frain*
frau, *deceit*	*frau*dulent
frus, ——	*frus*trate
frigi, *cold*	*frigi*d
frug, *fruit*	*frug*al
frui, ——	*frui*tful
fruc, ——	*fruc*tify
front, *the fore part*	*front*ispiece
frutes, *a shrub*	*frutes*cent
fuge, *to fly*	re*fuge*
fugi, ——	*fugi*tive
fus, *to pour*	in*fus*e
fut, ——	*fut*ile *
fund, ——	re*fund*
fulge, *to shine*	re*fulge*nt

* *Futile*, trifling; fit only to be poured out.

VERBAL ANALYSIS.

Roots and meanings.	Examples.
fulc, *a prop*	*fulc*rum
fund, *the bottom*	*fund*amental
found, ———	*found*ation
——— *to pour*	con*found*
furt, *a thief*	*furt*ive
fulmin, *lightning*	*fulmin*ate
fum, *smoke*	*fum*e
gen, *a family*	*gen*eration
— *nature*	*gen*erosity
— *disposition*	*gen*ius
— *to beget*	hydro*gen*
— *to act*	a*gen*t
ger, *to bear*	con*ger*ies
— *a bud*	*ger*m
ges, *to gather*	di*ges*t
geal, *frost, to congeal*	con*geal*
gela, ———	*gela*tinous
genu, *the knee*	*genu*flection
gesi, *ten times*	quadra*gesi*ma *
glaci, *ice*	*glaci*ers
grad, *a step*	*grad*ual
gress, ———	pro*gress*
gree, ———	de*gree*
grac, *favour, agreeableness, kindness*	*grac*ious
grat, ———————	*grat*ify
greg, *a flock*	congre*g*ate

* *Quadra*, four, *gesi*, ten times; hence *quadragesima* signifies forty.

Roots and meanings.	Examples.
gru, *a flock*	con*gru*ous
grav, *heavy; a weight*	*grav*ity
gramin, *grass*	*gramin*ious
gust, *taste*	dis*gust*
gutt, *a drop*	*gutt*er
gurg, *a bubbling, a whirlpool*	*gurg*ling
hab, *to have, to hold*	in*hab*it
hib, ——	pro*hib*it
hal, *to breathe*	in*hal*e
haust, *to drink up*	ex*haust*
her, *to stick*	ad*here*
hes, ——	ad*hes*ion
here, *an heir*	*here*ditary
hia, *to gape*	*hia*tus
hilar, *cheerful*	*hilar*ity
hom, *man*	*hom*icide
hort, *a garden*	*hort*iculture
—— *to persuade*	ex*hort*
horr, *to tremble*	*horr*id
horo, *an hour*	*horo*logy
hora, ——	*hora*ry
hos, *a guest*	*hos*pitable
—— *an army*	*hos*t
—— *an enemy*	*hos*tile
hum, *a man*	*hum*an
—— *the ground*	in*hum*e
—— *dampness*	*hum*id
jac, *to lie*	ad*jac*ent
jec, *to throw*	in*jec*t

Roots and meanings.   **Examples.**

Roots and meanings	Examples
jejune, *empty*	*je*june
igni, *fire*	*igni*te
imper, *empire*	*imper*ial
—— *command*	*imper*ative
impetu, *violence*	*impetu*ous
insul, *an island*	*insul*ar
ira, *anger*	*ira*scible
ire, ——	*ire*
incens, *to burn*	*incens*e
incend, ——	*incend*iary
jocu, *a joke*	*jocu*lar
iti, *a journey*	*iti*nerant
it, *to go*	trans*it*
jug, *to join*	con*jug*ate
joi, ——	con*joi*n
junc, ——	con*junc*tion
jut, ——	coad*jut*or
jus, *law, right*	*jus*tice
jur, *to swear*	*jur*y
jer, ——	de*jer*ation
juven, *young*	*juven*ile
jun, ——	*jun*ior
jubil, *to rejoice*	*jubil*ee
jurga, *to scold*	ob*jurga*tion
lact, *milk*	*lact*ary
lacer, *to tear*	*lacer*ate
lat, *to carry*	trans*lat*e
—— *side*	*lat*eral
—— *breadth*	*lat*itude

L 2

Roots and meanings.		Examples.
lat, *hidden*	....	*lat*ent
laps, *a slip or fall*	....	rel*aps*e
lips, ———	......	el*lips*is
lax, *loose*	....	re*lax*
lapid, *a stone*	......	*lapid*ary
laud, *praise*	....	*laud*able
lamb, *to lick*	....	*lamb*ient
lass, *weary*	....	*lass*itude
lachry, *a tear*	....	*lachry*mal
lan, *wool*	....	f*lan*nel
lab, *a lip*	....	*lab*ial
latr, *to bark*	......	*latr*ant
langu, *to faint*	.....	*langu*id
lev, *lightness*	......	*lev*ity
lief, *to lift*	....	re*lief*
les, *to choose, gather, read, send,*		
or leave ; law	....	*les*son
lec, ———	....	*lec*ture
leg, ———	......	de*leg*ate
— ———	......	*leg*al
lect, ———	......	e*lect*
— ———	......	de*lect*able
leni, *mild*	....	*leni*ent
liber, *to be free*	..	*liber*al
liba, *to pour*	......	*liba*tion
let, *a letter*	....	*let*ter
lit, ———	....	*lit*eral
libid, *lust*	....	*libid*inous
liqu, *to melt*	......	*liqu*ify

VERBAL ANALYSIS.

Roots and meanings.   **Examples.**

lig, *to bind*	*li*gature
libr, *a book*	*libr*ary
— *to weigh*	de*liber*ate
liri, *to fail*	de*liri*ous
lid, *to strike*	col*lid*e
lis, ——	col*lis*ion
line, *a line*	*lin*eament
lin, *flax*	*lin*en
limp, *clear*	*limp*id
lymph, *water*	*lymph*æduct
ligne, *wood*	*lign*eous
limen, *a threshold*	pre*limin*ary
litig, *to contend*	*litig*ate
loca, *a place*	*loca*l
long, *length*	*long*itude
locu, *to speak*	inter*locu*tory
loqu, ——	*loqu*acious
ling, *a language*	*ling*uist
lud, *to play*	*lud*icrous
lus, ——	col*lus*ion
lut, *to wash*	pol*lut*e
luv, ——	al*luv*ial
lav, ——	*lav*e
lot, ——	*lot*ion
lug, ——	de*lug*e
luc, *light*	*luc*id
lumi, ——	il*lumi*nate
luct, *to strive*	re*luct*ant
lux, *abundance*	*lux*ury

Roots and meanings.	Examples.
luna, *the moon*	*lu*natic *
lucra, *gain*	*lu*crative
lugu, *mourning*	*lugu*brious
magn, *great*	*magn*itude
major, *greater*	*majo*rity
mal, *bad*	*mal*ady
manu, *hand*	*manu*al
main, ——	*main*tain
—— *principal*	*main*ly
man, *to flow*	e*man*ate
mand, *to order*	de*mand*
mend, *or commit*	com*mend*
maci, *lean*	e*maci*ate
mari, *the sea*	*mari*ne
macula, *a stain*	im*macula*te
mam, *the breast*	*mam*milary
magistr, *a master or ruler*	*magistr*ate
marmor, *marble*	*marmor*ean
mater, *a mother*	*mater*nal
matr, *ripe*	*matr*on
matur, ——	*matur*ity
maxi, *a principle, great*	*maxi*m
—— *the jaw*	*maxi*liary
met, *to measure*	*met*re
mea, ——	*mea*sure
mensura, ——	*mensura*tion
medi, *the middle*	*medi*ator

* Persons out of their minds are worse at the changes of the moon than at other times; hence they are called lunatics.

Roots and meanings.	Examples.
meri, *the middle*	*meri*dian
merc, *to buy*	*merc*hant
— *to hire*	*merc*enary
mem, *to remember*	*mem*orial
merse, *to plunge*	im*merse*
merg, ——	e*merge*
menda, *falsehood*	*menda*city
mea, *to flow*	*mea*nder
mer, *pure*	*mer*e
— *the sea*	*mer*maid
meretri, *a lewd woman, alluring*	*meretri*cious
melior, *better*	*melior*ate
mephit, *stinking*	*mephit*ic
ment, *the mind*	*ment*al
mendi, *to beg*	*mendi*city
migra, *to remove*	*migra*te
min, *less*	*min*or
— *small*	*min*ute
— *to threaten*	im*min*ent
miss, *to send*	*miss*ion
mit, ——	com*mit*
mire, *to wonder*	ad*mire*
mira, ——	*mira*cle
mitig, *to soften*	*mitig*ate
miscu, *to mingle*	pro*miscu*ous
miser, *miserable*	com*miser*ate
minister, *a servant*	*minister*ial
molu, *gain, to heap*	e*molu*ment
mole, *to move*	*mole*st

Roots and meanings.	Examples.
moli, *to move*	de*moli*sh
mon, *to teach*	*mon*itor
— *to advise*	ad*mon*ish
— *to inform*	*mon*ument
mort, *death*	*mort*al
mot, *to move*	*mot*ion
mov, ———	*mov*eable
mom, ———	*mom*ent
molli, *soft*	e*molli*ent
morb, *disease*	*morb*id
modi, *a mode or measure*	*modi*fy
mur, *to delay*	de*mur*
— *a wall*	*mur*al
muni, *a gift*	*muni*ficent
— *free*	*muni*ciple
mult, *many*	*mult*itude
musi, *a song*	*musi*c
mut, *to change*	*mut*able
mund, *the world*	*mund*ane
— *clean*	*mund*atory
mun, *to converse*	com*mun*e
mulg, *to publish*	pro*mulg*e
— *to milk*	e*mulg*e
muls, ———	e*muls*ion
mulc, *to soothe*	de*mulc*ent
muriat, *brine, salt*	*muriat*e
muliebr, *a woman*	*muliebr*iety
mutu, *borrowed*	*mutu*al
nate, *born*	in*nate*

Roots and meanings.	Examples.
nati, *born*	*nation*
natu, —	*nature*
nas, *the nose*	*nasal*
nata, *to swim*	*natant*
naut, *a ship*	*nautical*
nav, —	*navigate*
narr, *to relate*	*narration*
nefar, *wicked*	*nefarious*
neg, *not*	*negative*
ne, —	*neuter*
n, —	*null*
nex, *to join or knit*	an*nex*
nec, —	con*nec*t
nemor, *a grove*	*nemor*is
nihil, *nothing*	an*nihil*ate
nici, *death*	per*nici*ous
nigr, *black*	de*nigr*ate
nidu, *a nest*	*nidu*late
niv, *to wink*	con*niv*e
— *to snow*	*niv*eous
not, *known*	*not*ation
— *marked*	de*not*e
— *numbered*	*not*ice
noc, *night*	*noc*turnal
— *guilt*	in*noc*ent
nox, *night*	equi*nox*
— *guilt*	*nox*ious
norm, *a rule, law*	e*norm*ous
nom, *a name*	*nom*inate

Roots and meanings.	Examples.
novem, *nine*	*N*ovember
nup, *marriage*	*nu*ptial
nub, ——	con*nub*ial
nun, *to declare or name*	an*nun*ciate
noun, ——	an*noun*ce
nony, ——	a*nony*mous
nutri, *to nourish*	*nutri*ment
nud, *naked*	*nud*ity
nubi, *a cloud*	*nubi*ferous
nebu, ——	*nebu*lous
occul, *to hide*	*occul*t
ocul, *the eye*	*ocul*ar
odi, *hatred*	*odi*ous
odo, *sweet*	*odo*rous
oli, *to grow*	ab*oli*sh
ole, ——	ad*ole*scence
ali, ——	co*ali*tion
ale, ——	co*ale*sce
ol, *to smell*	*ol*factory
ole, ——	grave*ole*nt
omni, *all, every*	*omni*present
oner, *a burden*	ex*oner*ate
onus, ——	*onus*
opt, *to wish*	*opt*ion
opu, *powerful*	*opu*lent
opin, *to think*	*opin*ion
opera, *a work*	*opera*tion
opa, *dark*	*opa*que
ori, *rising*	*ori*ent

Roots and meanings.	Examples.
ordi, *beginning*	prim*ordi*al
— *order*	sub*ordi*nate
ora, *to pray, to speak*	*ora*cular
ore, —	ad*ore*
orna, *to beautify*	*orna*ment
orb, *a globe*	*orb*icular
ossi, *a bone*	*ossi*fication
osten, *to show*	*osten*sible
otia, *leisure*	neg*otia*te *
ova, *an egg*	*ova*l
ovi, —	*ovi*parous
par, *to appear*	com*par*e
— *a part*	quadri*par*tite
— *to make ready*	pre*par*e
pair, —	im*pair*
pater, *a father*	*pater*nal
patr, —	*patr*onize
pass, *to suffer*	*pass*ion
pati, —	*pati*ence
paci, *peace*	*paci*fic
pand, *to open*	ex*pand*
peri, —	ex*peri*ence
pact, *an agreement*	com*pact*
patri, *one's own country*	*patri*ot
parv, *small*	*parv*ity
pauci, *few*	*pauci*ty
pauper, *poor*	*pauper*ism

* *Neg*, not, *otia*, leisure; hence negotiate signifies not at leisure, *i. e.* engaged in business.

Roots and meanings.	Examples.
partu, *to bring forth*	par*tu*rition
par, ———	ovi*par*ous
pala, *a palace*	*pala*tial
parsi, *to spare*	*parsi*mony
pasto, *to feed*	*pasto*r
pastu, ———	*pastu*re
petr, *a stone*	*petr*ify
pel, *to drive or compel*	ex*pel*
puls, ———	re*puls*e
peal, ———	re*peal*
pend, *to hang*	*pend*ant
pens, ———	*pens*ive
ped, *a foot*	im*ped*iment
peti, *to seek or desire*	*peti*tion
pete, ———	com*pete*nce
pen, *almost*	*pen*insula
—— *sorrow, punishment*	*pen*itence
pun, *punishment*	im*pun*ity
pecto, *the breast*	*pecto*ral
pecc, *sin*	*pecc*able
penetra, *to go through*	*penetra*te
pell, *the skin*	*pell*icle
pest, *a plague*	*pest*ilence
pecu, *a flock*	*pecu*liar
pi, *devout*	ex*pi*ate
—— *dutiful*	*pi*ous
pil, *hair*	*pil*osity
—— *a heap*	*pil*e
plain, *to make even*	*plain*

VERBAL ANALYSIS.

Roots and meanings.   **Examples.**

Root	Example
plau, *to praise*	ap*plaud*
plex, *to twist*	com*plex*
plen, *full,*	*plen*itude
ple, —	com*plete*
ply, *to bend or fold*	*pli*ant
plic, ——	sur*plice*
ply, ——	com*ply*
pla, *to please*	com*plaisant*
plac, —	im*plac*able
plor, *to search*	ex*plore*
— *to bewail*	de*plore*
plu, *more*	*plu*ral
pluv, *rain*	*pluv*ious
plum, *a feather*	*plume*
— *lead*	*plum*ber
pleb, *the common people*	*pleb*eian
pos, *to put or place*	de*pos*it
pon, ——	post*pone*
poun, ——	pro*pound*
popul, *people*	de*populate*
publ, —	*publ*ic
port, *to carry*	*port*able
— *a gate*	*port*al
pont, *a bridge*	*pont*oon
— *a high priest*	*pont*iff
pot, *power*	des*pot*
— *to drink*	*pot*ation
postul, *to demand*	ex*postul*ate
polle, *to be able*	equi*pollent*

Roots and meanings.	Examples.
pond, *a weight*	*ponderous*
proxim, *near*	*proximate*
prow, *the head*	*prowess*
prob, *to prove*	*probation*
— *honesty, sincerity*	*probity*
prehend, *to take*	*apprehend*
pregna, ———	*impregnable*
press, *to squeeze*	*compress*
preci, *to value*	*appreciate*
prav, *crooked*	*depravity*
prec, *to pray*	*deprecate*
preda, *prey, booty*	*depredation*
prim, *first*	*primary*
priv, *private*	*privilege*
prompt, *ready*	*promptitude*
pron, *bending, inclining*	*prone*
propri, *one's own*	*appropriate*
proca, *wanton*	*procacity*
premi, *reward*	*premium*
prodig, *enormous*	*prodigious*
proli, *offspring*	*prolific*
pruden, *knowledge, foresight*	*prudence*
putr, *rotten*	*putrid*
put, *to think*	*impute*
— *to cut off*	*amputate*
pung, *to prick*	*pungent*
punc, ———	*puncture*
pulchr, *fair*	*pulchritude*
puer, *a boy*,	*puerile*

VERBAL ANALYSIS.

Roots and meanings.	Examples.
purg, *to cleanse*	*purg*ative
pugna, *a fight*	re*pugn*ant
pulv, *powder*	*pulv*erize
pude, *modesty*	im*pud*ent
pube, *ripeness of age*	*pub*erty
pulmo, *the lungs*	*pulm*onary
qua, *to shake*	*qu*ake
cus, ———	con*cus*sion
quant, *as many as*	ali*quant* *
quadr, *four, equal*	*quadr*ant
quat, ———	*quat*ernion
quart, *fourth*	*quart*o
ques, *to seek, to ask*	*ques*tion
quies, *rest*	*quies*cent
queru, *to complain*	*queru*lous
quin, *five*	*quin*tuple
quot, *as many as*	ali*quot* †
rar, *thin*	*rar*ity
——— *uncommon*	*rar*e
radi, *a ray*	*radi*us
——— *a root*	*radi*cal
raz, *to rub out*	*raz*e
ras, ———	e*ras*e
ratio, *reason*	*ratio*nal
rati, *strong*	*rati*fy
rap, *to snatch*	*rap*acity
rep, ———	sur*rep*titious
rami, *a branch*	*rami*fy

* With a remainder.   † Without a remainder.

Roots and meanings.	Examples.
ramo, *a branch*	*ramose*
rect, *to govern*	*rectitude*
rig, ——	*right*
reg, ——	*regent*
reig, ——	*reign*
rept, *to creep*	*reptile*
redem, *to buy*	*redemption*
recen, *new*	*recent*
rig, *to water*	*irrigate*
rigi, *stiff*	*rigid*
rimo, *a chink*	*rimosity*
rit, *a ceremony*	*ritual*
risi, *laughter*	*risible*
rog, *to intreat*	*rogation*
—— *to demand*	*interrogate*
rod, *to gnaw*	*corrode*
robor, *to strengthen*	*corroborate*
rota, *a wheel*	*rotation*
rori, *dew*	*rorifluent*
rupt, *to break*	*rupture*
rud, *clownish, ignorant*	*rude*
rus, *the country*	*rustic*
rur, ——	*rural*
rubr, *red*	*rubric* *
rumin, *a cud*	*ruminate* †
sacr, *holy, holy places*	*sacred*

* A book of church laws; so called because they were formerly written in red ink. † When an ox is chewing the cud, he seems to be meditating; hence the derivation of this word.

VERBAL ANALYSIS.

Roots and meanings.	Examples.
secr, *holy, holy places*	secret
ecr, ——	execrate *
sacer, *a priest*	sacerdotal
sapi, *wise*	sapient
saga, ——	sagacity
san, *whole, healthy*	sanity
sangu, *blood*	sanguinary
salv, *to save, healing*	salvation
salu, ——	salutary
scintil, *a spark*	scintillation
scend, *to mount*	ascend
scent, ——	ascent
sci, *knowledge*	science
scrib, *to write or draw*	scribble
scrip, ——	subscription
scrut, *to search*	scrutiny
sculp, *to carve*	sculpture
sess, *to sit*	session
sed, ——	sedentary
sid, ——	consider
sent, *to think*	dissent
seni, *old*	senior
seri, *to sow or set in order*	series
sert, ——————	insert
semi, ——————	disseminate
serv, *to keep, to watch*	preserve
—— *a slave*	servitude
seve, *harsh*	severe

* Out of holy places, *i. e.* excluded from holy places

Roots and meanings.	Examples.
seren, *calm*	*seren*e
sere, *late*	*seren*ade
sex, *six*	*sex*tant
sept, *seven*	*sept*ennial
sepul, *to bury*	*sepul*chre
secul, *an age, time*	*secul*ar
simil, *like*	*simil*ar
simul, *together*	*simul*taneous
sist, *to fix*	con*sist*
stan, —	*stan*d
stab, —	e*stab*lish
stin, —	di*stin*guish
sta, —	*sta*bility
stit, —	con*stit*ute
siti, *thirst*	*siti*ent
sider, *a star*	*sider*al
silici, *flint*	*silici*ous
sinu, *a bay*	*sinu*ous
sip, *taste*	in*sip*id
sapo, —	*sapo*rific
— *soap*	*sapo*naceous
sicc, *dry*	*sicc*ous
singul, *alone*	*singul*ar
somn, *sleep*	*somn*iferous
soci, *a companion*	*soci*al
solv, *to loosen*	re*solv*e
solu, ——	*solu*tion
sol, *alone*	*sol*itude
— *the sun*	*sol*ar

Roots and meanings.	Examples.
sole, *to be accustomed*	ob*sole*te
son, *sound*	*son*orous
sorb, *to swallow*	ab*sorb*
sorp, ——	ab*sorp*tion
sord, *filth*	*sord*id
sopor, *sleep*	*sopor*ific
soror, *a sister*	*soror*icide
splend, *to shine*	*splend*id
spers, *to sprinkle*	a*spers*e
spoli, *to spoil*	*spoli*ation
spec, *to view*	in*spec*t
spic, ——	de*spic*able
spir, *to breathe*	in*spir*e
—— *to wind*	*spir*al
spou, *to promise*	e*spou*se
spon, ——	*spon*sor
—— *to answer*	re*spon*d
spont, *will, free*	*spont*aneous
spair, *hope*	de*spair*
sper, ——	de*sper*ation
spin, *a thorn*	*spin*ous *
spum, *froth*	*spum*e
squal, *filth*	*squal*id
squamo, *the scale of a fish*	*squamo*sity
struc, *to pile*	con*struc*t
stel, *a star*	*stel*lar
strain, *to bind*	con*strain*

* The back bone is called the spine, from its supposed resemblance to a thorn stick.

Roots and meanings.   **Examples.**

Root	Meaning	Example
strict,	to bind	s*trict*ure
string,	——	a*string*ent
stil,	to drop	di*stil*
stult,	foolish	*stult*ify
stip,	to condense	con*stip*ation
——	wages, bargain	*stip*ulate
strid,	to make a noise	*strid*ulous
strep,	——	ob*strep*erous
stern,	to throw	con*stern*ation
stimul,	a spur	*stimul*ate
stagna,	to stand still	*stagn*ant
sult,	to jump	con*sult*
sum,	to take	as*sum*e
sump,	——	as*sump*tion
surd,	deaf	ab*surd*
suag,	sweet	as*suag*e
suav,	——	*suav*ity
summ,	the highest	*summ*it
subli,	——	*subli*me
sudo,	sweat	*sudo*rific
sue,	to accustom	de*sue*tude
sui,	his own	*sui*cide
succu,	juice	*succu*lent
sur,	to rise	re*sur*rection
sut,	to sew	*sut*ure
sylva,	a wood	*sylva*n
tac,	to touch	con*tac*t
tig,	——	con*tig*uous
ting,	——	con*ting*ent

Roots and meanings.	Examples.
tang, *to touch*	*tang*ible
tag, ——	con*tag*ion
tard, *slow*	re*tard*
tamin, *to pollute*	con*tamin*ate
taci, *to be silent*	*taci*t
tali, *such*	re*tali*ate
tabula, *a table*	*tabula*r
tend, *to stretch*	*tend*ency
tens, ——	ex*tens*ion
ten, *to hold*	*ten*or
tain, —	re*tain*
tin, —	abs*tin*ence
test, *a witness, a proof*	*test*ator
temp, *time*	*temp*oral
— *a temple*	con*temp*late
— *to despise*	con*temp*t
— *to try*	at*temp*t
tenu, *thin*	at*tenu*ate
terr, *the earth*	sub*terr*anean
ter, ——	in*ter*
tex, *to weave*	*tex*ture
tect, *to cover*	pro*tect*
teg, ——	in*teg*ument
term, *a bound, a limit*	*term*inate
teri, *to rub or wear away*	de*teri*orate
trit, ——	*trit*urate
tere, *to bore*	*tere*brate
tep, *warm*	*tep*id
terg, *to cleanse*	de*terg*ent

Roots and meanings.	Examples.
terg, *the back*	*terg*iversation
testa, *a shell*	*testa*ceous
temer, *rash*	*temer*ity
till, *the earth*	*till*age
tinc, *a colour*	*tinc*ture
tin, ——	*tin*ge
tirp, *a root*	ex*tirp*ate
tim, *fear*	*tim*id
ton, *thunder*	de*ton*ate
tort, *to twist*	ex*tort*
tot, *so many*	*tot*al
torr, *to roast*	*torr*id
—— *a rushing steam*	*torr*ent
toler, *to bear*	*toler*ate
trac, *to draw*	re*trac*t
trib, *a race*	*trib*e
—— *a tax*	*trib*ute
trus, *to thrust*	in*trus*ion
trud, ——	pro*trud*e
tri, *three*	*tri*angle
trep, *to fear*	in*trep*id
trem, ——	*trem*ble
tric, *a net*	ex*tric*ate
trunc, *to lop*	de*trunc*ation
tum, *a swelling*	*tum*our
tus, *to bruise*	con*tus*ion
tuiti, *to see*	in*tuiti*on
turb, *a whirlpool*	*turb*ulent
uber, *fruitful* | ex*ub*erance |

Roots and meanings.	Examples.
ult, *the last*	*ult*imate
— *to jump*	ex*ult*
ul, *any*	nu*ll*
umbr, *shade*	*umbr*ageous
uni, *one*	*uni*ty
und, *a wave*	abo*und*
uple, *fold*	quint*uple*
urb, *a city*	sub*urb*s
uter, *either*	ne*uter*
uti, *use*	*uti*lity
unc, *to anoint*	*unc*tion
uvid, *wet*	*uvid*ity
uxor, *a wife*	*uxor*ious *
vacc, *a cow*	*vacc*ination
vail, *to be well*	a*vail*
val, *to be worth*	*val*ue
— *to be strong*	*val*iant
vast, *to waste*	de*vast*ation
vagr, *to wander*	*vagr*ant
vad, *to go*	in*vad*e
vas, —	in*vas*ion
vac, *empty*	*vac*uity
ven, *to come*	con*ven*e
— *to sell*	*ven*dor
vers, *to turn*	con*vers*e
vert, —	in*vert*
— *the top*	*vert*ical
vestig, *to trace*	in*vestig*ate

* Submissively fond of a wife.

Roots and meanings.	Examples.
veri, *true*	*veri*fy
vera, —	*vera*city
velo, *swift*	*velo*city
verd, *green*	*verd*ure
ver, *spring*	*ver*nal
veter, *old*	*veter*an
vet, *to forbid*	*vet*o
vehi, *to draw*	*vehi*cle
veni, *pardon*	*veni*al
vent, *the belly*	*vent*riloquist
— *the wind*	*vent*ilate
verm, *a worm*	*verm*icular
ver, —	cada*ver*ous
verg, *to shoot*	di*verg*e
vest, *to clothe*	in*vest*
verber, *a stroke*	re*verber*ate
vesper, *evening star*	*vesper*s *
vesi, *a bladder*	*vesi*cle
verb, *a word*	*verb*al
vid, *to see*	e*vid*ent
vis, —	*vis*ual
vic, *to conquer*	*vic*tory
vanq, —	*vanq*uish
vinc, —	in*vinc*ible
— *to bind*	*vinc*ture
viv, *to live*	re*viv*e
vit, —	longe*vit*y †
via, *a way*	*via*duct

* Evening prayer. † Or rather from *eva*, an age.

VERBAL ANALYSIS.

Roots and meanings.	Examples.
vio, *a way*	*per*vio*us*
vice, *a deputy, in place of*	*vice*roy
vigil, *to watch*	*vigil*ant
vibr, *to move*	*vibr*ate
vigor, *to flourish*	*vigor*ous
viscer, *entrails*	*viscer*a
vindic, *to avenge*	*vindic*ate
vir, *a man*	*vir*ility
vici, *change*	*vici*ssitude
vicin, *a neighbour*	*vicin*ity
vitri, *glass*	*vitri*fy
voli, *to wish*	*voli*tion
vole, *to will, to fold*	*bene*vole*nt*
volu, ——	*volu*ntary
volv, *to roll, to fold*	*re*volv*e*
valv, ——	*valv*es
vor, *to devour*	*vor*acious
vola, *to fly*	*vola*tile
vow, *to utter, to promise*	*a*vow
vok, *to call, to speak*	*con*vok*e*
voc, ——	*voc*ative
voic, ——	*voic*e
void, *empty*	*a*void
vuls, *to pluck*	*con*vuls*e*
vulg, *the common people*	*vulg*ar
—— *to noise abroad*	*di*vulg*e*
vulner, *a wound*	*in*vulner*able*

VERBAL ANALYSIS.

Roots and meanings.	Examples.

ROOTS FROM THE FRENCH.

bar, *a defence*	*bar*gain
beau, *handsome*	*beau*tiful
bord, *brink, edge*	*bord*er
burs, *a purse*	dis*burs*e
cher, *dear*	*cher*ish
champ, † *a field*	*champ*aign
chute, *a fall*	para*chute*
clar, *bright*	*clar*ify
coy, *to shut up*	*coy*ish
cuit, *to bake*	bis*cuit*
daunt, *to subdue*	un*daunt*ed
dam, *loss*	*dam*age
dress, *to make straight*	re*dress*
egar, *sour*	vin*egar*
foss, *to dig*	*foss*dike
fort, *strong*	*fort*itude
franc, *free*	*franc*hise
fusil, ‡ *a hand gun*	*fusil*ier ‖
gaunt, *a glove*	*gaunt*let
gage, *to pledge*	en*gage*
gros, *thick*	*gros*s
grap, *a cluster*	*grap*ple
jour, *a day*	ad*jour*n
lit, *a bed*	*lit*ter
lish, *to lick*	re*lish*
lieu, *instead of*	*lieu*tenant

† Pron. shamp. ‡ Pron. fuzee. ‖ The *l* is pronounced.

VERBAL ANALYSIS.

Roots and meanings. **Examples.**

matin, *morning* .... *matins*
maraud, *to plunder* .. *marauder*
mass, *a heap* ...... a*mass*
mena, *to threaten* .... *menace*
mode, *fashion, form* .. *modern*
nov, *new* .... *novel*
œuvre, † *a work* .... man*œuvre*
parl, *to talk* ...... *parley*
poise, *to weigh* .... equi*poise*
reve, *a dream* ...... *reverie*
roy, *a king* ...... vice*roy*
rodo, *to wander* .... *rodomontade*
semble, *like, to seem* .. re*semble*
sue, *to follow* ...... pur*sue*
tant, *so much* ...... *tantamount*
tire, *to draw* ...... re*tire*
toil, *to clothe* ...... *toilet*
trench, *to cut* ...... re*trench*
velop, *to cover* .... en*velope*
vin, *wine* ...... *vinegar*

ROOTS FROM OTHER LANGUAGES.

coil, *to strike, to wind* .... re*coil*
gor, *blood* .... *gore*
hoar, *white* .... *hoary*
hoc, *high* .... *hoc*tide

† Pron. uvr.

Roots and meanings.	Examples.
meni, *servants*	*me*ni*al*
mach, *a contrivance*	*mach*ine
neal, *to breathe*	an*neal*
pascha, *a passage*	*pascha*l
tide, *time*	hoc*tide*
ward, *a defence*	out*ward*

WORDS.

As the following words would not easily admit of being analyzed, they are given entire.

MONOSYLLABLES.

Bane, *poison, mischief*
Blithe, *merry*
Bourn, *a boundary, a brook*
Carp, *to find fault; the name of a fish*
Choir (pronounced quire), *a band of singers*
Chaste, *pure*
Couch, *to lie down; a kind of sofa*
Coif, *a hood or cap*
Cone, *a figure rising from the circumference of a circle to a point*
Cruise, *to sail*
Cube, *a solid of six square sides*
Dawn, *beginning*
Deign (pron. dane), *to condescend*
Dearth, *a scarcity*
Disk, *face of the sun or moon*
Dire, *dreadful*
Dirge, *a funeral song*
Feud (pron. fewd), *a quarrel*
Fiend (pron. feend), *an evil spirit*
Filch, *to steal*
Film, *a thick skin*
Garb, *dress*
Gauge (pron. gage), *to measure*

Gaunt (pron. gant), *lean*
Germ, *a bud*
Gird, *to tie round*
Glebe, *soil*
Gleam, *a streak of light*
Goad, *to spur on*
Gorge, *to glut*
Guile, *fraud, deceit*
Haunch, *the thigh*
Keel, *the bottom of a ship*
Knell, *the toll of a bell*
Knead, *to work dough*
League (pron. leeg), *an agreement*
Loan, *a thing lent*
Lurk, *to lie hid*
Maim, *to wound*
Mosque (pron. mosk), *a Turkish or Mahometan temple*
Mound, *a bank*
Mulct, *a fine*
Myrrh, *a perfume*
Niche (pron. nitch), *a place in a wall for a statue*
Orb, *a ball, a circle*
Pawn, *to pledge*
Phlegm (pron. flem), *spittle, coldness, dulness*
Pulp, *a soft substance*

Quack, *a pretender*
Quaff, *to drink*
Qualm (pron. quarm), *faintness*
Quash (pron. quosh), *to overthrow*
Raft, *a frame of timber*
Schism (pron. sizm), *a division*
Skiff, *a small boat*
Sledge, *a carriage without wheels*
Slough (pron. slo), *a muddy place*
Sluice, *a vent for water*
Smirk, *a pleasant look*
Sock, *a high shoe formerly worn by comic actors*
Spa or Spaw, *a mineral water*
Spawn, *the eggs of fish*
Spleen, *ill humour*
Suit, *a petition*
Suit (pron. sweet), *a set*
Stole, *a state robe*
Swain, *a shepherd*
Taint, *to infect*
Taunt, *to insult*
Tithe, *a tenth*
Thwart, *to oppose*

Tour (pron. toor), *a journey*
Trait (pron. tray), *an outline*
Trite, *common*
Type, *a printing letter, an emblem*
Vague, *unmeaning*
Vaunt, *to boast*
Vase (pron. vaws), *an urn*
Vault (pron. volt), *an arch*
Veer, *to change*
Verge, *brink, edge*
Vie, *to contend*
Wag, *a merry fellow*
Wane, *decrease*
Wreck, *destruction*
Yacht (pron. yot), *a pleasure boat*
Yoke, *a bond*
Yore, *of old time*
Zest, *relish*

WORDS ACCENTED ON THE FIRST SYLLABLE.

Abbot, *the governor of an abbey*
Abbess, *the governess of a nunnery*
Abbey, *a religious society among the Roman Catholics*
Acme, *height*
Ægis, *the shield of Pallas, a goat*
Amble, *to pace*
Amber, *a fragrant gum*
Arctic, *northern; the constellation called the Bear*
Argil, *clay*
Atlas, *a book of maps*
Ballot, *to vote by tickets or balls*
Beacon (pron. beekon), *a public signal*
Bias, *bent, inclination*
Billow, *a wave*
Bigot, *a superstitious person*
Broker, *one who transacts business for others*
Buckler, *a shield*
Budget, *a bag*
Bulwark, *a defence*
Burgess, *a freeman*
Buskin, *a high shoe formerly worn by tragic actors*
Butler, *a head servant*
Buttress, *a prop*
Callous, *gristly, insensible*

Callow, *unfeathered*
Cancel, *to blot out*
Casemate, *a platform*
Canvas, *to solicit; a coarse cloth*
Chaplet (pron. tshaplet), *a wreath*
Chattels (pron. tshattels), *goods*
Churlish (pron. tshurlish), *surly*
Citron, *a small kind of lemon*
Classic, *an author of the first rank*
Combat, *a battle*
Comment, *explanation*
Crisis (pron. krysis), *a critical point of time*
Cutler, *a knife-maker*
Damask, *flowered silk*
Dexter, *right, fortunate*
Diet, *food; an assembly, or continental parliament*
Dogma, *positiveness, an opinion*
Drama, *a play*
Echo, (pro. ekko) *the sound returned or repeated*
Epic, *heroic*
Era, *an age, a particular date*
Ethic, *moral*
Fibre (pron. fiber), *a fine thread*
Florid, *red, blooming*
Focus, *the burning point*
Foible, *a weakness*
Forage, *provisions*
Foster, *to nurse, to cherish*
Frolic, *a merriment*
Function, *duty*
Garble, *to sift*
Gamut, *a scale of music*
Gargle, *to wash the throat*
Garnish, *to adorn*
Gallant, *brave*
Ghastly, *pale*
Gothic, *ancient*
Gormand, *a glutton*
Grovel, *to be mean or contemptible*
Halo, *a ring*
Harpy, *a snatcher*
Havoc, *slaughter, destruction*
Hallow, *to make holy*
Heathen (pron. heethen), *an idolater, i. e. one who worships idols*

Hectic, *consumptive*
Hector, *to boast*
Heinous (pron. haynous), *enormous*
Hero, *a brave man*
Hover, *to hang about*
Idol, *an image, a false god*
Irony, *contrary to the meaning*
Lavish, *to waste*
Legend, *a fable*
Libel, *a lie*
Lustre, *brightness*
Lyre, *a kind of harp*
Magic, *conjuration*
Magnet, *a loadstone*
Mammon, *the god of wealth and worldly things*
Mantle, *a cloak*
Marvel, *to wonder*
Massy, *solid*
Maxim, *a principle*
Martial, *warlike*
Miasm, *infectious particles floating in the air*
Mitre, *a bishop's crown*
Mortgage, *land security*
Motley, *mixed*
Motto, *a short sentence*
Morass, *a marsh*

Nectar, *drink of the gods*
Nitre, *saltpetre*
Noisome, *loathsome*
Nurture, *support*
Omen, *a sign*
Orphan, *destitute*
Ordnance, *heavy cannon*
Ordure, *filth, dung*
Overt, *acting in an open manner*
Pagan, *a worshipper of idols*
Papist, *a Roman Catholic*
Palate, *the sense of taste*
Pallid, *pale*
Peasant, *a countryman, a labouring man*
Pedant, *a pretender*
Phœnix (pron. fenix), *a fabulous bird*
Pirate, *a sea robber, a literary thief*
Plaintiff (pron. planetif), *complainant*
Poignant (pron. poinant), *sharp*
Proxy, *a deputy*
Purport, *meaning*
Quagmire, *a bog*
Quiver, *a case for arrows*

Rabid, *mad*
Rampant, *wanton, a beast raised on its hind legs*
Rancour, *malice*
Ransome, *to redeem*
Ravage, *to waste*
Rostrum, *a kind of pulpit*
Rigid, *strict*
Satire, *ridicule*
Sarcasm, *a satirical jest*
Sceptic or skeptic, *a doubter*
Schedule (pron. sedjule), *a paper, a list*
Scion, *a shoot*
Scruple, *to doubt*
Shambles, *butcher's stalls*
Shrivel, *to wrinkle*
Silex, *flint*
Skirmish, *a slight engagement*
Solace, *comfort*
Sqeamish, *delicate, sickly*
Stagnant, *standing still*
Styptic, *to stop blood*
Stoic, *insensible*
Statute, *an act of parliament, a written law*
Steril, *barren*
Sterling, *real*
Stigma, *a mark of infamy*
Sturdy, *strong, hardy*
Suffrage, *a vote*
Sultan, *an emperor*
Swaddle, *to wrap up*
Symbol, *an emblem*
Synod, *an assembly of divines*
Syringe, *a squirt*
Tabor, *a small hand drum*
Talon, *a claw*
Tamper, *to meddle*
Taper, *a thin candle*
Target, *a shield*
Terrace, *a raised way*
Testy, *peevish*
Thraldom, *slavery*
Tittle, *a small particle*
Topic, *an argument*
Traffic, *trade*
Tranquil, *quiet*
Trophy (pron. trofy), *a token, an emblem*
Turgid, *puffed up*
Turret, *a little tower*
Tyro, *a beginner, a learner*
Vanish, *to dissappear*
Vapid, *flat*
Vassal, *a slave*
Vellum, *parchment made of calf-skin*
Viand, *food*

Victim, *a sacrifice*
Viol, *a fiddle*
Viscous, *clammy*
Visor or vizard, *a mask*
Umpire, *a judge*
Utter, *to speak*
Wallet, *a bag*
Wicket, *a small gate*
Wrangle, *to quarrel*
Yeoman, *a farmer*
Zero, *a cypher, as* 0
Zenith, *the point overhead*
Admiral, *a naval commander*
Alcohol, *spirit of wine*
Alcali, *an antiacid*
Amputate, *to cut off*
Amethyst, *a violet-coloured stone*
Anchorite (pron. ankoret), *a hermit*
Boronet, *a title next to a lord*
Bagatelle (pron. bagatel), *a trifle*
Beverage, *drink*
Botany, *the knowledge of plants*
Calumny, *slander*
Diocess, *the jurisdiction of a bishop*

Dialect, *the peculiar language of a province or county*
Diadem, *a crown*
Dissipate, *to dispense*
Document, *a precept, instruction, a written paper*
Dynasty, *a race of kings*
Elegy, *a funeral song*
Element, *a first principle*
Empiric, *a quack*
Emerald, *a green stone*
Embassy, *a state message*
Epicure, *a luxurious person*
Eucharist, *the Lord's supper*
Fascinate, *to bewitch*
Fealty, *duty, homage*
Feasible, *likely*
Finical, *foppish*
Garrison, *a fortified place*
Gorgeous, *showy*
Halcyon (pron. halshion), *calm, serene*
Harbinger, *a forerunner*
Heresy, *an opposite opinion*
Homily, *a discourse*
Infantry, *foot soldiers*
Jubilee, *a celebration*
Labyrinth, *a maze, a puzzle*

VERBAL ANALYSIS.

Laity, *people not clergymen*
Larceny, *petty theft*
Litany, *a supplication*
Liturgy, *common prayer*
Mansion, *a large house*
Meteor, *a luminous body*
Minion, *a favorite*
Miscreant, *a wretch*
Mutilate, *to mangle, to destroy*
Mutiny, *a riot*
Myriad, *ten thousand*
Notary, *a public writer*
Nunnery, *a house for nuns*
Overture, *a proposal*
Palliate, *to lessen*
Palpable, *evident, sensible to the touch*
Palpitate, *to beat*
Parapet, *a wall breast-high*
Pageant, *a pompous show*
Policy, *prudence, government, a warrant for money*
Presbyter, *an elder of the church*
Proselyte, *a convert*
Protocol, *a first or rough copy*
Puritan, *a dissenter from the church*
Remnant, *a remainder*
Recipe, *medical prescription*
Regimen, *diet*
Renegade, *an apostate, one who deserts*
Ribaldry, *loose language*
Satiate, *to fill*
Scrivener, *a writer for hire*
Secular, *worldly*
Sensitive, *feeling*
Servitor, *one of the lowest rank at college*
Simony, *unlawfully trafficking in church preferment*
Sinister, *the left, bad, unfair*
Solecism, *an impropriety*
Stratagem, *an artful invention*
Subsidy, *a tax, a supply*
Summary, *short*
Surrogate, *a deputy*
Sumptuary, *relating to expenses*
Sycophant, *a flatterer*
Tantalize, *to tease*
Tapestry, *needlework covering for walls*
Termagant, *a scold*
Theory, *speculation, supposition*

Titular, *having the name only*
Treachery, *deceit, want of faith*
Virulent, *hurtful, violent*
Vitiate, *to corrupt*
Usury, *money-lending*

WORDS ACCENTED ON THE SECOND SYLLABLE.

Achieve, *to accomplish*
Appal (pron. appaul), *to terrify*
Arraign (pron. arrane), *to accuse*
Assail, *to attack*
Bouquet (pron. bokay), *a nosegay*
Brigade, *a party of soldiers*
Burlesque (pron. burlesk), *to ridicule*
Cabal, *a faction, a party*
Cajole, *to flatter*
Caprice (pron. caprees), *whim*
Career, *a course*
Carouse, *to drink hard*
Cartel (pron. carteel), *an exchange of prisoners of war*
Cashier (pron. casheer), *a cash-keeper, to discharge*
Chicane (pron. shekane), *a trick*
Chagrin (pron. shagreen), *vexation*
Congee, *a bow, a curtsey*
Dismay, *a terrifying*
Dispatch, *to hasten*
Divorce, *to separate*
Dragoon, *a horse soldier*
Eclat (pron. eclaw), *show, lustre*
Eclipse, *to darken*
Elope, *to run away*
Embalm, *to preserve dead bodies*
Facade (pron. fasade), *a front*
Finance, *revenue*
Forlorn, *forsaken*
Fracas (pron. fracaw), *a squabble*
Gangrene, *a mortification*
Gallant, *polite to females*
Gazette, *a newspaper*
Instate, *to put in possession*
Obscure, *dark*

VERBAL ANALYSIS.

Parterre, (pron. partare) *a flower garden*

Parole, *word, or word of honour*

Patrol, *men who keep watch on horse-back*

Poltroon, *a coward*

Profile (pron. profeel), *side face*

Purloin, *to steal*

Remorse, *sorrow*

Rebuke, *to reprove*

Renown, *fame*

Reprieve, *a pardon*

Requite, *to reward*

Retrieve, *to regain*

Revere, *to venerate*

Revolt, *to rebel*

Sojourn, *to tarry*

Supine, *careless*

Suborn, *to procure false witnesses*

Usurp, *to take illegally*

Abdomen, *the belly*

Abortive, *before the time, unsuccessful*

Arcanum, *a secret*

Bravado, *a boasting*

Bitumen, *pitch*

Chimera, *a wild fancy*

Disciple, *a learner, a follower*

Enigma, *a riddle*

Extinguish, *to put out*

Exotic, *foreign*

Histrionic, *belonging to the stage*

Idea, *an image in the mind*

Laconic, *short*

Purveyor, *a provider*

Quandary, *a doubt, a perplexity*

Refection, *a refreshment*

Sedition, *a tumultuous uproar*

Statistics, *resources of a country*

Artillery, *heavy cannon*

Battalion, *a body of soldiers*

Carrillions, *chimes*

Calamity, *trouble, misfortune*

Discomfiture, *overthrow*

Escutcheon, *coat of arms, a shield*

Palladium, *a safeguard*

Pavillion, *a state tent, a pleasure house*

Phenomenon, *an appearance in nature*

Punctilio, *great nicety*
Repudiate, *to separate*
Rotundity, *roundness*
Scurrility, *low language*
Tribunal, *a seat of justice*
Tautology, *a repetition*

Thadolite, *an instrument for taking angles*
Volcano, *a burning mountain*
Urbanity, *good breeding*

WORDS ACCENTED ON THE THIRD SYLLABLE.

Buccanier (pron. buccaneer), *an American pirate*
Gasconade, *to boast*
Idoneus, *fit, proper*
Interloper, *an intruder*
Quarantine, (pron. quaranteen), *forty days*

Rendezvous (pron. rondevoo), *a place of meeting*
Repartee, *wit, a smart reply*
Reconnoitre, *to observe, to view*

PHRASES.

FOREIGN WORDS AND PHRASES IN COMMON USE.

Aid de camp (aid de cong), *assistant to a general*
A la mode (aw la mode), *fashionable*
Apropos, (awpropo), *to the point*
Argent comptant (aurzshong kongtong), *ready money*
Beau monde (bo mond), *fashionable world*

Belles lettres (bel laytur), *polite literature*
Bon mot (bong mo), *wit*
Bonne bouche (bong bush), *a nice morsel*
Bon ton (bong tong), *fashion*
Boudoir (boodwr) *a small private apartment*
Carte blanche (cartblansh) *unconditional terms*

PHRASES.

Chateau (shato) *country seat*

Chef d'œvre (sha doover), *a master-piece*

Ci-devant (see-devaung), *formerly*

Comme il faut (com e fo), *as it should be*

Con amore (con amo-re), *gladly*

Conge d'elire (congee de leer), *permission to choose*

Cordon (cordong), *a line*

Corps (core), *a body*

Corps diplomatique (*— diplomawteek), *the diplomatic body*

Coup de grace (coo de grass), *finishing stroke*

Coup de main (coo de main), *sudden enterprise*

Coup d'œil (coo dail), *glance*

Debut (dabu), *beginning*

Denouement (dennoomong), *finishing*

Dernier (dernya), *last*

Depot (deepo), *store, magazine*

Dieu et mon droit (dew a mong drwau), *God and my right*

Double entendre (doobl ontongder), *double meaning*

Douceur, (dooseur), *present, bribe*

Droit des gens (— da zhong), *the right of nations*

Du fort au foible (du fort o foibl), *from the strong to the weak*

Eleve (elave), *pupil*

En bon point (ong bong pwong), *jolly*

Enfans perdus (ongfong perdu), *lost children*

Enfan gate (—gawtay), *spoiled children*

En flute, (—flute), *carrying guns on the upper deck only*

En masse (—mass), *in a mass*

*A dash placed as above, shows that the pronunciation of that word has been given in a previous phrase.

En passant (—passong), *by the way*

En plein jour (—plain zure), *in open day*

Entre (ongtray), *entrance*

Entre nous (—noo), *between ourselves*

Esprit de corps (espree—), *spirit of the party*

Faux pas (fo paw), *misconduct*

Fete champetre (fate shaungpaytur), *a rural feast*

Gaiete de cœur (gayatay de cur), *gaiety of heart*

Gens de l'eglise (dshong de l'egleeze), *churchmen*

Gens de guerre (—gare), *military men*

Gens de condition (—condisyong), *men of rank*

Haut gout (hoo go), *high flavour*

Haut ton, *first fashion*

Honi soit qui mal y pense (honey sow ke mal a pons), *evil to him who evil thinks*

Hors de combat (hors de congbaw), *out of condition to fight*

Ich dien (ik dean), *I serve*

Je ne sais quoi (dshen e sa qwar), *I know not what*

Jeu de mots (dshew de mow), *a play upon words*

Jeu d'esprit, *a play of wit*

L'argent (lardshong), *silver money*

L'empire des lettres (lompeer —), *the republic of letters*

Le roi et l'etat (ler waw a la taw), *the king and the state*

Mal a propos (mol aw propo), *unseasonably*

Mauvaise honte (movays hont), *over bashfulness*

Mots d'usage (—d'swash) *common phrases*

Nom de guerre (nong de gare), *assumed name*

Non chalance (— shalawnce), *indifference*

On dit (wong dee) *they say*

Outre (ootray), *preposterous*

Perdue (perdue), *concealed*

Petit maitre (petty maytur), *a fop*

Point d'appui (pwong dopwee), *basis*

Protege (protezhay), *a person protected*

Rouge, (roodzsh), *red, red paint*

Ruse de guerre (rus de gare), *a stratagem*

Sang froid (song froaw), *coolness*

Sans, *without*

Sauve qui peut (sove ke poo), *save himself who can*

Savant, (savang), *a learned man*

Soi-disant (swaw deesong), *pretended*

Tapis (toppee), *carpet*

Trait (tray), *feature*

Tel maitre, tel valet (tel mayter, tel vala), *like master, like man*

Tete a tete (tate aw tate), *face to face*

Unique (uneek), *singular*

Valet de chambre (— shawm), *a footman*

Verite sans peur (veretay song poor), *truth without fear*

Vive la bagatelle, (veve la bagatel), *success to trifles*

Vive le roi, *long live the king*

LATIN PHRASES IN COMMON USE.

[*Ti* and *ci* before a vowel are pronounced like *she*: as, ab initio—*ab inisheo.* Final vowels are always sounded.]

Ab initio, *from the beginning*

Absit invidia, *without envy*

Ad arbitrium, *at pleasure*

Ad captandum, *to attract*
Addenda, *to be added*
Ad eundem, *to the same*
Ad honores, *for decency's sake*
Ad infinitum, *to infinity*
Ad libitum, *at pleasure*
Ad referendum, *for consideration*
Ad valorem, *according to value*
Affirmatim, *in the affirmative*
A fortiori, *with stronger reason*
Agenda, *things to be done*
Alias, *otherwise*
Alibi, *elsewhere*
Alma mater, *university*
Amor patriæ, *love of our country*
A mensa et thoro, *from bed and board*
Anglice, *in English*
A posteriori, *from the latter, behind*
A priori, *from the former, first*
Arcana imperii, *state secrets*
Arcana, *a secret*
Argumentum ad hominum, *personal argument*
Argumentum baculinum, *argument of blows*
Argumentum ad ignorantium, *a foolish argument*
Argumentum ad judicium, *argument to the judgment*
Assumpsit, *it is assumed*
Audi alteram partem, *hear both sides*
Bona fide, *in reality*
Bonus, *a benefit*
Cacoethes scribendi, *fondness for writing*
Capias, *permission to take*
Caput mortuum, *the thick matter which remains after distillation*
Certiorari, *to be made more certain*
Communibus annis, *one year with another*
Compos mentis, *of sound mind*
Credat Judæus, *a Jew may believe,* or *can a Jew believe?*
Contra bonos mores, *against good manners*

Copia verborum, *a variety of words*
Cui (ki) bono, *to what good will it lead?*
Cui malo, *to what harm?*
Cum multis aliis, *with many others*
Cum privilegio, *with privilege*
Custos morum, *the guardian of morality*
Custos rotulorum, *keeper of the rolls*
Datum, *a settled point*
De facto, *in fact*
Dei gratia, *by the grace of God*
De jure, *by right*
De novo, *anew*
Deo favente, *with God's favour*
Deo juvante, *with God's assistance*
Deo volente, *God willing*
Desideratum, *a thing desired*
Desunt cœtera, *the rest is wanting*
Divide et impera, *divide and govern*
Dictum, *said*
Domine dirige nos, *O Lord direct us*
Dominus providebit, *the Lord will provide*
Dramatis personæ, *characters represented*
Dum vivimus vivamus, *whilst we live, let us live*
Durante bene placito, *during pleasure*
Durante vita, *during life*
Ecce signum, *behold an example*
Ecce homo, *behold the man*
Ergo, *therefore*
Erratum, *an error*
Errata, *errors*
Esto perpetua, *may it last for ever*
Ex, *late*
Ex curia, *out of court*
Excerpta, *extracts*
Ex concesso, *from what has been granted*
Ex officio, *by virtue of office*
Ex parte, *on one side*
Fac simile, *exact copy*
Felo de se, *self-murder*

Fiat, *let it be done*
Fieri facias (fasheas), *cause it to be done*
Fugam fecit, *he has taken to flight*
Finis, *the end*
Gratis, *for nothing*
Habeas corpus, *have the body*
Homo multarum literarum, *a man of various learning*
Hora fugit, *time flies*
Ibidem, *in the same place*
Idem, *the same*
Id est, *that is*
Idoneus homo, *a fit man*
Imperium in imperio, *a government in a government*
Imprimatur, *let it be printed*
Imprimis, *in the first place*
Impromptu, *in readiness*
In cœlo quies, *rest in heaven*
Incognito, *unknown*
In commendum, *for a time*
In conspectu fori, *in the eyes of the law*
In curia, *in the court*
In forma pauperis, *as a pauper*
In foro conscientiæ, *at the tribunal of conscience*
In loco, *in the place*
In posterum, *for the time to come*
In petto, *kept back*
In propria persona, *in person*
In statu quo, *in the former state*
Internos, *between ourselves*
In terrorem, *as a warning*
In transitu, *on the passage*
In toto, *altogether*
Ipse dixit, *mere assertion*
Ipso facto, *by the fact itself*
Item, *also, an article*
Judicium Dei, *the judgment of God*
Jure divino, *by divine right*
Lapsus linguæ, *slip of the tongue*
Lex non scripta, *the unwritten law*
Lex terræ, *the law of the land*
Lex scripta, *the written law*

Lex talionis, *the law of retaliation*
Literati, *men of learning*
Locum tenens, *a deputy*
Magna charta (karta), *the great charter of England*
Major domo, *the manager of a house*
Malum in se, *a thing evil in itself*
Memento mori, *remember that thou must die*
Memoriter, *by rote*
Meum et tuum, *mine and thine*
Minimum, *the least*
Minutiæ, *minute concerns*
Mirabile dictu, *wonderful to tell*
Mittimus, *we send*
Multum in parvo, *much in little*
Mutatis mutandis, *changing words*
Necessitas non habet legem, *necessity hath no law*
Nemine contradicente, *without opposition.*—nem. con.
Nemine dissentiente, *without dissent*
Nemo me impune lacesset, *nobody shall provoke me with impunity*
Ne plus ultra, *nothing beyond the truth*
Ne quid nimis, *pursue not any object too far*
Ne tentes aut perfice, *attempt not or accomplish*
Nolens volens, *willing or not*
Nolo episcopari, *I do not wish to be made a bishop*
Non compos mentis, *not of sound mind*
Non nobis solum, *not for ourselves alone*
Nosce te ipsum, *know thyself*
Nota bene, *mark well*
O tempora! o mores! *oh! the times, oh! the manners*
Omnes, *all*
Onus probandi, *the burden of proving*
Passim, *every where*
Per se, *by itself*
Pinxit, *painted it*
Posse comitatus, *the power of the country*
Postulata, *points assumed*

Præcognita, *previously known*
Prima facie, *on the first face or view*
Primum mobile, *the first mover*
Pro aris et focis, *for our altars and our fire-sides*
Probatum est, *it is approved*
Pro et con, *for and against*
Pro bono publico, *for the public good*
Pro forma, *for form's sake*
Pro hac vice, *for this turn*
Pro rata, *in proportion*
Pro re nata, *for a special thing*
Pro tempore, *for the time*
Quam diu se bene gesserit, *so long as he shall behave well*
Quantum sufficit, *a due proportion*
Quis capit ille facit, *let him wear the cap whom it fits*
Quid nunc, *what now*
Qui separabit, *who shall separate us?*
Qui tam, *an information on a penal statute*
Quo animo, *with what mind?*
Quo ad, *as to*
Quondam, *former*
Quorum, *a sufficient number*
Quo warranto, *by what authority*
Regium donum, *the king's gift*
Res publica, *the common weal*
Rex, *king*
Regina, *queen*
Requiescat in pace, *rest in peace*
Resurgam, *I shall rise again*
Scandalum magnatum, *scandal against the great*
Scripsit, *wrote it*
Sculpsit, *engraved it*
Semper eadem, *always the same*
Seriatim, *in regular order*
Sic passim, *so every where*
Sine die, *without naming a day*
Sine qua non, *nothing without that*
Sine invidia, *without envy*

Sine odio, *without hatred*
Spectus et tu spectabere, *you see and will be seen*
Status quo ante bellum, *the state before the war*
Sub pœna, *under a penalty*
Sub silentio, *under silence*
Succedaneum, *a substitute*
Sui generis, *singular*
Suggestio falsi, *suggestion of a falshood*
Summum bonum, *the highest good*
Supersedeas, *you may remove or set aside*
Tempus edax rerum, *time devours all things*
Tempus fugit, *time flies*
Tempus omnia revelat, *time reveals all things*
Tertium quid, *a third thing*
Toto corde, *with the whole heart*
Tria juncta in uno, *three joined in one*
Tuum est, *it is your own*
Ubi supra, *where above mentioned*
Una voce, *with one voice*
Utile dulci, *utility with pleasure*
Uti possidetis, *each retaining what he has gained*
Ut supra, *as above*
Ut infra, *as below*
Vade mecum, *constant companion*
Veluti in speculum, *as in a looking-glass*
Veni, vidi, vici, *I came, I saw, I conquered*
Verbatim, *word for word*
Veritas vincit, *truth conquers*
Versus, *against*
Veto, *I forbid*
Via, *by the way of*
Vice, *in place of*
Vice versa, *the reverse*
Vide, *see*
Vide et crede, *see and believe*
Viva voce, *by word of mouth*
Vivant, *live*
Vulgo, *vulgarly*
Vox populi, *the voice of the people*

ABBREVIATIONS.

A. B. or B. A. bachelor of arts
A. D. in the year of our Lord
A. M. before noon, master of arts, the year of the world
A. U. C. in the year of Rome
B. D. bachelor of divinity
B. M. bochelor of medicine
D. D. doctor of divinity
F. A. S. fellow of the antiquarian society
F. L. S. fellow of the Linnæan society
F. R. S. fellow of the royal society
F. S. A. fellow of the society of arts
W. R. King William
K. B. knight of the bath
K. G. knight of the garter
J. H. S. Jesus the saviour of men
L. C. lord chancellor
L. C. J. Lord cheif justice
L. L. D. doctor of laws
M. A. master of arts
M. D. doctor of medicine
M. P. member of parliament
M. S. sacred to the memory of
MS. manuscript
MSS. manuscripts
N. B. take notice
N. S. new stile
P. M. afternoon
Q. E. D. which was to be demonstrated
Q. E. I. which was to be discovered
R. king or queen
St. saint or street
Bart. baronet
Capt. captain
Co. company
Do. ditto, as before
Esq. esquire
Gent. gentleman
Genl. general
Gov. governor
Gr. gross
Hon. honorable
Hond. honoured

Knt. knight
Lieut. lieutenant
Messrs. or M. M. sirs
No. number
P. S. postcript
e. g. for example
q. d. as if he should say
i. e. that is
id. the same
ib. in the same place
v. verse
Fol. folio

4to. quarto
8vo. octavo
12mo. duodecimo
Xmas. Christmas
Mmas. Michaelmas
&. and
&c. and so forth
1st. first
2d. second
3d. third
4th. fourth, &c.

ARITHMETICAL TABLES, &c.

NUMERATION.

Units 1
Tens 21
Hundreds 321
Thousands 4,321
Tens of thousands 54,321
Hundreds of thousands 654,321
Millions 7,654,321
Tens of millions 87,654,321
Hundreds of millions 987,654,321
Billions 9,087,654,321
Tens of billions 90,807,654,321
Hundreds of billions 908,070,654,321

Any number of figures may be numerated by dividing it into triplets or threes, and by adding *llions* or *illions* to Latin numerals: as, tri*llions*, quadr*illions*, quint*illions*, sext*illions*, &c.

The following Latin numerals may be joined to *llions* or *illions*: *bi, tri, quadr, quint, sext, sept, oct, non, dec, undec, duodec.*

MULTIPLICATION TABLE.

	2	3	4	5	6	7	8	9	10	11	12
1	2	3	4	5	6	7	8	9	10	11	12
2	4	6	8	10	12	14	16	18	20	22	24
3	6	9	12	15	18	21	24	27	30	33	36
4	8	12	16	20	24	28	32	36	40	44	48
5	10	15	20	25	30	35	40	45	50	55	60
6	12	18	24	30	36	42	48	54	60	66	72
7	14	21	28	35	42	49	56	63	70	77	84
8	16	24	32	40	48	56	64	72	80	88	96
9	18	27	36	45	54	63	72	81	90	99	108
10	20	30	40	50	60	70	80	90	100	110	120
11	22	33	44	55	66	77	88	99	110	121	132
12	24	36	48	60	72	84	96	108	120	132	144

FARTHINGS.

Q.	D.	Q.	D.	Q.	D.	Q.	D.
4 are	1	16 are	4	28 are	7	40 are	10
8	2	20	5	32	8	44	11
12 —	3	24 —	6	36 —	9	48 —	12

PENCE.

D.		S.	D.	D.		S.	D.		S.
20	are	1	8	12	are	1	144	are	12
30	—	2	6	24	—	2	156	—	13
40	—	3	4	36	—	3	168	—	14
50	—	4	2	48	—	4	180	—	15
60	—	5	0	72	—	6	192	—	16
70	—	5	10	84	—	7	204	—	17
80	—	6	8	96	—	8	216	—	18
90	—	7	6	108	—	9	228	—	19
100	—	8	4	120	—	10	240	—	20
				132	—	11			

SHILLINGS.

S.		£.	S.	S.		£.	S.	S.		£.	S.
20	are	1	0	80	are	4	0	500	are	25	0
30	—	1	10	90	—	4	10	600	—	30	0
40	—	2	0	100	—	5	0	700	—	35	0
50	—	2	10	200	—	10	0	800	—	40	0
60	—	3	0	300	—	15	0	900	—	45	0
70	—	3	10	400	—	20	0	1000	—	50	0

S.	D.		S.	D.	
2	6	half a crown	10	0	half a sovereign
5	0	a crown	20	0	a sovereign
10	6	half a guinea	6	8	a noble
21	0	a guinea	13	4	a mark

ARITHMETICAL CHARACTERS.

\+ Plus.—The sign of Addition.

— Minus.—The sign of Subtraction.

× Multiply by.—The sign of Multiplication.

÷ Divide by.—The sign of Division.

= Equal to.

: Is to.

: : As.

$\frac{12}{4}$ Shews that 12 is to be divided by 4.

$\sqrt{}$ Square root.

$\sqrt[3]{}$ Cube root.

If the last figure of any number be even, the whole will divide by 2 without a remainder.

If the two last figures will divide by 4 without a remainder, the whole will divide by 4 without a remainder.

If the three last figures will divide by 8 without a remainder, the whole will divide by 8 without a remainder.

If the last figure be a 5 or an 0, the whole will divide by 5.

If the sum of any number of figures will divide by 9 or 3, the whole will divide by 9 or 3.

PRACTICE TABLES.

Of a Pound.

s.	d.			s.	d.		
10	0	is	½	3	4	—	1-6th
6	8	—	1-3d	2	6	—	1-7th
5	0	—	1-4th	2	0	—	1-10th
4	0	—	1-5th				

ARITHMETICAL TABLES.

Of a Shilling

D.			D.		
6	is	½	2	—	1-6th
4	—	1-3d	1½	—	1-8th
3	—	1-4th	1	—	1-12th

Of a Hundred-Weight.

QRS.			LBS.		
2	is	½	16	is	1-7th
1	—	1-4th	14	—	1-8th

Of a Quarter.

LBS.			LBS.			LBS.		
14	is	½	7	is	¼	4	is	1-7th

WEIGHTS AND MEASURES.

CONTRACTIONS.*

gr. grain
dwt. pennyweight
oz. ounce
℈ scruple
ʒ dram, *apothecaries' weight*
℥ ounce, *ibid.*
℔. pound
dr. dram, *avoirdupoise weight*
qr. quarter
cwt. hundred weight
t. ton

nl. nail
yd. yard
F. e. Flemish ell
E. e. English ditto
Fr. e. French ditto
b. c. barley corns
in. inch
ft. foot
fath. fathom
a. acre
rd. rood
r. rod
p. poll or perch

* The contractions should be used only as references, when the pupil is committing the tables of weights and measures to memory.

foth. fother
m. mile
lea. leauge
o. degree
′ minute
″ second
‴ third
cir. circle
s. sign
qt. quart
gal. gallon
an. anchor
run. rundlet
tie. tierce
hhd. hogshead
pp. pipe
bt. butt
firk. firkin
kil. kilderkin
bar. barrel
pun. puncheon
pot. pottle
pk. peck

bush. bushel
fur. furlong
str. strike
c. coomb
sk. sack
ch. chaldron
hr. hour
d. day
wk. week
mh. month
yr. year
sq. square
cub. cubic
trs. truss
ld. load
lin. lines
lk. link
cha. chain
wt. weight
mea. measure
hf. half
gl. gill

Troy weight.
24 gr . . . . 1 dwt
20 dwt . . . . . . 1 oz
12 oz . . . . 1 lb

Apothecaries' weight.
20 gr . . . . 1 ℈

3 ℈ . . . . 1 ʒ
8 ʒ . . . . 1 ℥
12 ℥ . . . . 1 ℔

Avoirdupoise weight.
16 dr . . . . 1 oz
16 oz . . . . 1 lb

ARITHMETICAL TABLES.

28 lb ....1 qr
4 qr ....1 cwt
20 cwt.........1 ton

Cloth measure.

2½ in ......1 nl
4 nl ....1 qr.
3 qr ....1 F. e.
4 qr ....1 yd
5 qr ....1 E. e
6 qr ....1 Fr. e

Long measure.

12 ln or 3b. c ..1 in
12 in..........1 ft
3 ft..........1 yd
6 ft or 2yd ..1 fath
5½ yd .....1 r or p
4 p..........1 cha
40 p..........1 fur
8 fur ....1 m
3 m ....1 lea
60 geographical or
69½ English m 1°
11 hf. yd or
16½ ft ......1 r or p
100 lk ....1 cha
80 cha ......1 m
1776 yd ....1 m
4 in ....1 hand

Square measure.

144 sq. in ......1 sq. ft
9 sq. ft ......1 sq.yd
30¼ sq. yd .. 1r or p
16 p. or 22 yd..1 cha
40 p ....1 rd
4 rd ....1 a
640 a ....1 m
100 ft..........1 sq.of
flooring
160 r ....1 a
4840 yd ....1 a
10 cha.........1 a

Cubic or solid measure.

1728 in ....1 ft
27 ft ....1 yd
166 3-8ths yd ..1 p
6400 p..........1 fur
512 fur ....1 m

Wine measure.

4 gl ....1 pt
2 pt ....1 qt
4 qt ....1 gal
10 gal 1 ank of brandy
18 gal ..... 1 run
31½ gal 1 bar or hf·hhd
63 gal ......1 hhd

84 gal ...... 1 pun
2 hhd .... 1 pp. or bt
2 bt .... 1 tun
4 hhd ...... 1 tun
252 gal .... 1 tun
126 gal .... 1 hhd

Ale and Beer measure.

2 pt .... 1 qt
4 qt .... 1 gal
8 gal .. 1 firk. of ale
9 gal .. 1 firk. of beer
2 firk .... 1 kil
2 kil .... 1 bar
1½ bar ...... 1 hhd
2 bar ...... 1 pun
2 hhd ...... 1 bt
54 gal ...... 1 hhd

Dry measure.

2 pt ...... 1 qt
2 pt .... 1 pot
4 qt .... 1 gal
2 gal ...... 1 pk
2 pk .... 1 bush
2 bush ...... 1 strk
4 bush ...... 1 c
2 c .... 1 qr
5 qr .... 1 wey
2 wey ...... 1 last

8 bush ...... 1 qr

Coal measure.

4 pk ...... 1 bush
3 bush ...... 1 sk
12 sk .... 1 chal
36 bush ...... 1 chal
21 chal ...... 1 score

Time.

60 ''' .... 1 ''
60 '' .... 1 '
60 ' .... 1 hr
24 hr .... 1 d
7 d .... 1 wk
4 wk ...... 1 mh
13 mh. 1 d. 6 hrs or
365 d. 6 hr .... 1 yr

Motion.

60 ''' .... 1 ''
60 '' .... 1 '
60 ' .... 1°
360° .... 1 cir
30° .... 1 s
12 s .... 1 cir

Hay.

60 lb of new hay or
56 lb of old hay 1 tr

36 tr.........1 ld

Wool.

28 lb ....1 tod
13 tod ....1 pack

Evolution.

The square of 1 is 1
— 2 — 4
— 3 — 9
— 4 — 16
— 5 — 25
— 6 — 36
— 7 — 49
— 8 — 64
— 9 — 81

The cube of 1 is 1
— 2 — 8
— 3 — 27
— 4 — 64
— 5 — 125
— 6 — 216
— 7 — 343
— 8 — 512
— 9 — 729

12 articles 1 dozen
12 dozen 1 gross
20 articles 1 score
5 score 1 common hund.
6 score 1 great hundred
24 sheets of paper one qr.
20 quires 1 ream
21½ qrs 1 printer's ream

Foreign money in sterling value.

	s.	D.
A French franc..........	0	10 1-8th
A French livre	0	10
A Spanish pistole	16	9
A Spanish ducat	6	9
A Spanish dollar	4	6
A Spanish piastre	3	7
A Spanish rial	0	5 3-8th
A Flemish ducat	9	3
A Flemish florin	1	3

		s.	d.
A German rix dollar......		3	8
A Portuguese moidore	£1	7	0
A Portuguese crusade		2	3
A gold rupee........	£1	15	0
A silver rupee		2	6
A pagoda		8	9
An Arabian piastre		4	6

One hundred thousand rupees are one lack.

The pound avoirdupoise is equal to 1 lb. 2 oz. 11 dwt. and 16 gr. troy.

When a figure stands alone, or in the first place on the right hand, it is called its simple value, but in every other place it is called its local value; i. e. the value that it derives from its situation.

The number of days in each month versified.

Thirty days hath September,
April, June, and November,
February hath twenty-eight alone,
And all the rest have thirty-one,
Except in leap-year, then's the time
February's days are twenty-nine.

A TABLE OF WORDS FOR ANALYZATION.

Acrimony	Animate	Anabaptist	Canticle
Acrimonious	Annals	Anachronism	Capacity
Acidity	Annual	Analysis	Captivate
Acidulate	Anniversary	Anthology	Captivity
Acute	Anterior	Antipodes	Conception
Acutely	Antecedent	Apologue	Conceive
Acumen	Antemeridian	Aristocracy	Capital
Action	Aquatic	Astrology	Chromatic
Actor	Aqueduct	Astronomy	Cautious
Actress	Arbitrator	Atmosphere	Concede
Active	Arbitrary	Autocrat	Concession
Actively	Ardent	Belligerent	Celerity
Activeness	Arduous	Benign	Celebrity
Actual	Artist	Benediction	Censure
Actually	Artisan	Benefaction	Censor
Aviary	Artificial	Benefit	Concern
Agent	Artless	Barometer	Citation
Agile	Artful	Bibliographer	Circulate
Agility	Auditory	Bibliomaniac	Civilian
Agitation	Audible	Biography	Clamour
Alias	Augment	Brachygraphy	Clarify
Alien	Acoustics	Brontology	Conclude
Alienate	Aerology	Casualty	Conclusion
Amatory	Aeromancy	Casuist	Cacophony
Amour	Aeronaut	Cadaverous	Caligraphy
Amorous	Agamist	Cascade	Catalogue
Amiable	Amphibious	Concise	Cenotaph
Atheist	Amphiscii	Concision	Chronic

Chronology	Dejection	Election	Extirpate
Chronometer	Depart	Elevate	Endemic
Climate	Distract	Elocution	Epidemic
Cultivate	Disinter	Elucidate	Epilogue
Culinary	Displease	Elude	Eulogy
Copious	Decagon	Emanate	Euphony
Cupidity	Decalogue	Emancipate	Filial
Cordial	Democracy	Emerge	Folio
Concord	Diagonal	Emotion	Fraction
Corporeal	Diagram	Equator	Fratricide
Corpulent	Dialogue	Equilateral	Genuflection
Corpse	Diameter	Equinoctial	Gravity
Corpuscle	Diapason	Eradiation	Genealogy
Credit	Diaphonous	Eradicate	Genithleology
Credulous	Diaphragm	Erudition	Geography
Creation	Dilemma	Evade	Geometry
Concrete	Diphthong	Event	Homicide
Curious	Dissyllable	Evident	Human
Cursory	Doxology	Evolution	Helioscope
Concur	Eccentric	Exasperate	Hemisphere
Concourse	Edict	Excite	Heptarchy
Diction	Edification	Exculpate	Heterodox
Dictate	Edify	Exert	Heterogeneous
Dictator	Effect	Exhaust	Hexagon
Dignity	Effulgent	Exonerate	Hippodrome
Durable	Egotism	Expectorate	Homogeneous
Duration	Egregious	Expedite	Horoscope
Donation	Egress	Expire	Hydraulics
Docility	Eject	Expletive	Illusion
Deject	Elate	Extempore	Imminent

WORDS FOR ANALYZATION.

Impede	Invocation	Obstreperous	Precede
Impel	Involve	Obstruct	Precise
Implicate	Ichthyology	Obtrude	Prelude
Impute	Journal	Occident	Prerogative
Incarnation	Lunatic	Occult	Prescience
Incendiary	Lexicography	Occur	Procrastinate
Incident	Lithography	Ocular	Proscribe
Incision	Mediterranean	Omission	Provide
Inculcate	Miracle	Omnipotence	Postpone
Indubitable	Mission	Omnipresence	Panacea
Induce	Microcosm	Omniscience	Pandæmonium
Infatuate	Megacosm	Opponent	Pandemic
Influence	Melody	Opportunity	Panoply
Infuse	Metachronism	Octagon	Ponorama
Innate	Metaphor	Oligarchy	Pantheon
Insinuate	Metropolis	Ornithology	Parachronism
Inspire	Microscope	Orthodox	Paradox
Instil	Misanthropist	Orthography	Paragraph
Instruct	Misogamist	Perambulation	Paraphrase
Integer	Monarch	Perceive	Pathetic
Intercede	Monogram	Perfect	Patriot
Interdict	Monologue	Perforate	Pedagogue
Interjection	Mythology	Perjure	Pentagon
Interregnum	Obdurate	Permit	Pericranium
Interrupt	Object	Persist	Perioeci
Intervene	Oblation	Perspective	Periscii
Intestate	Obliterate	Perspiration	Philanthropy
Introduce	Obloquy	Pervade	Phraseology
Invade	Obnoxious	Pervert	Planet
Invert	Obituary	Plenipotentiary	Planisphere

Pleonism	Redemption	Scanning	Supercede
Pneumatology	Redundancy	Secede	Superfluity
Polygamy	Reflux	Seclude	Superlative
Polygramma	Refractory	Secure	Superscribe
Polyglot	Refund	Select	Superstructure
Polypus	Refute	Semicircle	Snpervene
Polytheism	Reject	Sequel	Supervisor
Prochronism	Relapse	Sinecure	Sarcophagus
Prognostic	Relate	Soliloquy	Stenography
Programme	Relax	Subject	Symmetry
Prologue	Reluctant	Subjugate	Symphony
Protomartyr	Remit	Subjunctive	Sympathy
Prototype	Remunerate	Submit	Synchronism
Pseudoapostle	Repel	Subscribe	Synonyme
Pseudodox	Reprobate	Subsequent	Tantamount
Pseudomartyr	Reputation	Subsist	Tergiversation
Pseudophrophet	Resign	Substance	Terraqueous
Pyrometer	Respect	Subterfuge	Terrestrial
Ratio	Resplendent	Subtract	Testimony
Ratiocination	Resurrection	Suffer	Traduce
Radical	Retain	Suffusion	Transact
Rebellion	Retort	Support	Transcend
Recapitulate	Revert	Superannuate	Transcribe
Recede	Revive	Supplicate	Transfer
Recite	Revoke	Suppose	Transfuse
Reclaim	Revolve	Surface	Transgress
Recline	Rogation	Surmise	Translucid
Recollect	Rudiments	Surreptitious	Transmarine
Record	Rhetoric	Susceptibility	Translate
Redeem	Sacrifice	Sustain	Transmigration

Transmission	Tautology	Thermometer	Ubiquity
Transpire	Telegraph	Topography	Ventriloquist
Transport	Telescope	Triphthong	Verdict
Transpose	Theism	Trisyllable	Vocation
Tachygraphy	Theocracy	Typography	Vulnerable

ORTHOGRAPHY.

The letters within parentheses, in the following exercises, are those which must be inserted in the words that immediately follow them. For instance, (*b*) in the first exercise must be placed before *t* in debt. In the third exercise long *a* is expressed in the words by *aa*, one *a* must therefore be dropt. *Shun* is given as the sound of *tion*, *lis* for *lice*, *i* and *ee* for *ie*, &c. The letters in parentheses are therefore to be considered as guides to the orthography of the words at the head of which they stand.

The letters of the alphabet are divided into vowels and consonants. *A, e, i, o, u,* and *w* and *y*, when they begin a word or syllable, are vowels; the rest are consonants.

Two vowels form a diphthong; three a triphthong.

Dipthongs are proper when both the vowels are sounded, and improper when but one vowel is sounded.

SILENT LETTERS.

Supply the silent letters omitted in the following words.

1. (*b*) Det, dout, dum, clīm,[a] cōm, crum, thum, plum,[b] lam, lim, sutle, dellium, num, (*c*) musle, indīt, vituals, zar, zarina, sene, sent,[c] septre, sience, asend, desend, transend, (*ch*) sedule, sism, yat, (*d*) hansome, hankerchief, hansel, grounsel, fielfare, knowlege, (*g*) phlem, nat, new, ensin, benīn, nash, sīn, condīn, rein,[d] impūn, nomon, desīn, forein, oppūn, arrain, poinant, (*gh*) neibourly, rīteous, fīting, thout, līt, nīt, slīt, strait,[e] rīt,[f] delīt, tīt, freit, frit, slauter, wei,[g] hi,[h] sīt,[i] ni, althou, nei, si, hauty, eity, aut, (*h*) Tomas, tyme, astma, Tames, eir, erb, our,[j] onest, onour, ostler, umble, umour, rubarb, retoric, rapsody, reumatism, Hanna, halleluja, Messia, agast.

2. (*k*) Napsack, nee, now, night,[k] new,[l] nob, nucle, nowlege, navery, nit, not,[m] nife, nave,[n] (*l*) samon, coud, woud, shoud, chadron, mamsey, (*n*) hym, condem, autum,[o] colum, contem, (*s*) ile, iland, vicount, aile, Carlile, (*w*) hō, hōm, hose, rite[p] right,[q] rath, rong, ren, retch, ry, rist, rinkle, rangle, blo, cro, mo, hole,[r] rap, rought, anser, arro, sord, reck, holesome, rapper, ritten, (*p*) salm, temt, tolemy, emty, redemtion, attemt, contemt, exemt, salmist, salter, shaw, receit, rasberry, semstress, (*u*) gild,[s] gard, gardian, gess, gilt,[t] gide, bilt, plage, leage, teage, vage, (*t*) hasen, lisen, moisen, thisle, episle, aposle, casle, brisle, busle, ofen, sofen, erran, Chrismas, chesnut, hosler, morgage, bankrupcy, misletoe, ecla, hauboy, (*z*) rendevous.

[a] The long sound of a vowel, in these exercises, is denoted by - drawn across it. [b] Lead. [c] A smell. [d] To rule. [e] Not crooked. [f] Not wrong. [g] To balance. [h] Lofty. [i] A seeing. [j] A division of time. [k] A title. [l] Did know. [m] A fastening [n] A rogue. [o] When another syllable is added the *n* is sounded: as, Autumnal. [p] With a pen [q] A workman. [r] Not broken. [s] A fraternity. [t] Sin.

SOUNDS OF THE LETTERS.

All silent letters are in italics.

3. (*a*) Haate, hawll,[a] kaat, bawld, bawll,[b] cawll, fawll, gawll, pawll, skawld, baabe, baade, smawll, stawll, tawll, shawll, wawll, eclaw*t*, ceder, yo*ch*t, polsy, thrawldom, gro*n*e, (*e*) wee, pritty, thare, whare, repleete, secreet, sereene, seveere, rondzevous, simily, ceedar, Inglish, feemale, preecept, charactar, obs*u*rved, bettur, adheerent, (*i*) miind, merth, macheene, bombazeene, magazeene, thurd, ferst, berth, ferm, gurd, gurt, gurl, skert, wherl, burch, burd, durt, shurt, thurst, rudement, posseble, mareene, archetect, confedence, defenite, earleness, prodegy, regecide, regester, resedence, vigelant, stirrup contageon, decysive, horyzon, vertue, humanety, charety, generosety, sensebilety, happeness, sentements, lavesh, reprehenseble, precareous, peculear, pereod, vicissetude, origenal, adminester.

4. (*o*) Secund, souldier, stumach, trowphy, growcer, nun*e*, luse, tum*b*, du, tu, muve, pruve, nunsuit, uther, uven, phantum, poortrait, proofile, Rume, whum, wum*b*, cume, impruve, dune, blazen, culur, culumn, duing, duzen, guvern, grooss, sum*e*, irun, pruve, luve, abandun, abuve, (*u*) langwish, Thersday, pewmice, excheqwer, *rh*oobarb, rewbric, mermer, ewse, bisy, bisness, bery,[c] brewise, booll, trewant, rewmour, scriptzure, screwple, shugar, shure, minewte, minet*e*, ewserp, adjewtant, luxshury, hewman, lewcid, serplice, perswade, servive, tortchere, injer*e*, (*y*) copeist, christal, cilinder, mistery, proselite, piramid, stiptic, sistem, tirant, sillable, tiranny, beastle, brawne, martir, mertle.

5. (*c*) Rekluse, kourse, rekruit, sukseed, suksess, ansestor, insite,[d] presede, presise, proseed, resess, resite, reklaim, kalm, kopper, kut, sentre, sity, sy-

---

[a] A large room. [b] A round substance. [c] To inter. [d] To stir up.

press, kloy, kry, kalsine, konsede, konsise, deside, dissern, sivil, konfidense, krokodile, dissipline, ekstasy, fassinate, frolik, isikle, intrikate, laserate, medisine, spesify, suiside, visinage, absense, aksent, kansel, kandour, kaptain, kandle, chansel, sinder, sipher, sirkle, sirkuit, desent, dosile, duktile, dulset, sausepan, sauser, sausy, merser, prinsess, resent, reskue, skrawl, skribble, sekant, ulser, unkle, adjasent, assension, dissiple, eksentric, elisit, exkressense, explisit, imbesile, abstrakt, akt, mimik, eksel, afflikt, forse, pease, aksident, akkord, akkustom, akknowledge, aktive, aksent.

6. (*g*) Game, got, gun, jem, jiant, jipsum, adjitate, rejency, rejicide, rejester, vejetable, vijilent, jeorjic, jibbet, jimcrack, jinjer, jingle, oranje, pidjeon, selvaje, verjer, courajeous, rijid, (*h*) hwet, hwich, hwo, hwat, hwether, (*j*) halleluyah, (*l*) armond,[a] carm, barm, psarm, arms,[b] stawk, tawk, wawk, fawcon, chawk, bawk, carf, harve, (*s*) Mozes, ssister, ssizzors, dezign, rezign, chozen, raizin, bruize, chaize, chazm, noize, poize, prize, proze, raize, crimzon, comprize, dizmal, dezert, dezign, dezzert,[c] devize, diffuze, dizplace, dizarm, dizeaze, dizguize, dispoze, dizzolve, uze,[d] encloze, peazant, pheazant, phyzic, peruze, rezound, rezult, rezide, rezign, rezist, rezort, rezume, revize, premize, egotizm, equipoize, hezitate, peruzal, (*w*) renoun, (*p*) cubboard, (*x*) Zenophon, compleks, egsert, egsample, ekstricate, luksury, indeks, syntaks, teksture.

7. (*ch*) Tsursh, ake, shaise, tshain, arkangel, eko, poatsher, ostritsh, skolar, shandelier, shevalier, artshed, artsher, artshery, artsh-enemy, Tshisshester, karacter, Enok, tshapman, kemist, shagrin, tshange, skeme, teatsh, Arkepelago, artshbishop, arkeives, kyle, stomak, distik, detatsh, mashine, tshaste, naumaky,

[a] L is by no means silent in the above words, *al* having the sound of *ah* or *ar*. [b] Charitable donations. [c] Fruit, &c. after dinner. [d] When a verb.

arkitect, batshelor, catekise, mikaelmas, monark, patriark, sepulkre, tshalise, tshancel, tshaplain, marshioness, batsh, bleatsh, blotsh, breatsh, atsheive, (*gh*) couf, touf, enouf, trouf, draft, lauf, toufer, dou, brīt, ruf.

8. (*ph*) Fial, fisic, samphire, seraf, serafim, zefer, filip, nefew, Steven, blasfeme, atmosfere, emfasis, epitaf, metafer, paragraf, parafrase, frase, sofist, sycofant, camfor, cifer, fesant, fantom, trofy, orfan, sulfer, triumf, (*qu*) kwart, kwestion, conker, likor, (*al*) bawk, tawk, chawk, stawk, wawk, (*au*) cawght, cawse, clawse, frawd, gawze, hawl, pawse,[a] sawce, tawght, fawlt, sawsepan, sawser, sawcy, sawnter, sawsage, slawghter, vawlt, awnt, flawnt, gantlet, jandice, gawdy, gager, hawty, hotboy, nawty, pawper, plawdit, landry, lorel, lodanum, applawd, Awgust, awthor, awtumn, cawdle, cawtion, dawter, dant, exhawst, awgment, (*aa*) Aron, Isac, Canan.

9. (*ai*) Layd, ordayn, remayn, repayr, restraynt, sustayn, upbrayd, swayn, vayn, wayt, agenst, assayl, detayn, disdayn, maintayn, rayn,[b] rayse,[c] sayl,[d] saynt, slayn, snayl, sprayn, strayn, strayt,[e] fayl payl[f] plad, agen, rallery, fountayn, Britan, ayd, ayl,[g] aym, ayr,[h] bayl, bayt, brayn, chayn, chayr, chase, claym, drayn, frayl, faynt,[i] fayr,[k] fayth, flayl, gayn, gayt,[l] grayn, hayl,[m] hayr,[n] jayl, mayd,[o] mayl,[p] mayn,[q] nayl, payd, payn,[r] paynt, playn,[s] playt,[t] prayse,[u] rayl,[v] afrayd, wayst,[w] wayter, playntive, traytor, waynscot, proclaym, baliff, bargan, captin, certen, chaplin, curten, daynty, dayry, daysy, fayrly, portrayt.

10. (*ea*) Weel,[x] wreek,[y] wreeth, speer, steel,[z] steem,

---

[a] To stop. [b] Water from the clouds. [c] To lift up. [d] Of a ship. [e] Not crooked. [f] A bucket. [g] To be ill. [h] The atmosphere. [i] To be languid. [k] Not foul. [l] Manner of walking. [m] Frozen rain to salute. [n] Of the head. [o] A female. [p] Armour, carriage of letters. [q] Chief, principal. [r] Aching. [s] Clear. [t] A fold. [u] Commendation. [v] A fence. [w] Part of the body. [x] A rising on the skin. [y] To revenge. [z] To thieve.

206 ORTHOGRAPHY.

streek, streem, tee, teech, teese, veel, see,[a] seel,[b] seem,[c] seet, sheeth, sheer,[d] smeer, sneek, peel,[e] pleed, pleese, preech, reech, reed,[f] reem, screem, kneed,[g] leed, leek,[h] leeve, meed,[i] meel, meen,[k] peech, peek, appeer, beever, meet,[m] heer,[n] breethe, breth, medow, tresure, bred,[o] bare,[p] brake, grate,[q] pare,[r] sweer, teer, weer, breech,[t] beed, beek, beem, been,[u] bleek, ceese, cheep, cheet, cleen, cleer, cleeve, creem, creek, deel, dreem, eech, eest, feest, gleem, bredth, brest, clense, ded, def, derth, deth.

11. Erl, ern, erth, hed, helth, herd,[v] herse, lern, ment, perl, relm, serch, spred, sted, stelth, swet, thred, thret, tred, welth, yern, red,[w] reer, bereeve, bohee, conceel, ceese, deceese, pleese, impeech, wreeth, repeel, repeet, deecon, erly, fether, heven, jelous, redily, trechery, treeson, weery, wether,[x] beedle, beegle, beeker, bleech, brekfast, clenly, cleever, creeture, deer, dred, dreery, eeger, eegle, ernest, eesy, eet,[y] heet, feer, feeture, greese, heethen, hevy, leef, leen, lether, leven, meesles, mesure, neer, neet, pesant, phesant, plesure, redy, treecle, week,[z] weesel, zelous, zeel, medow, sergent, threten.

12. (*ei*) Highten, heress, leesure, seeze, surfit, waygh, vayn, daygn, ither, nither, forfit, forign, faygn, conceet, faynt,[1] here, raygn,[2] rayn,[3] theer,[4] vayl,[5] seeze,[6] ceeling, tint, conceeve, deceet, deceeve, receeve, nayhbour, aght, frayt, haynous, hefer, (*eo*) infeff, peeple, jepardy, lepard, feffment, dungen, sturgen, surgen, punchen, yoman, bludgen, (*eu*) Urope, Uclid, fewd, rhoom, grandjer, newtral, (*ey*) pray,[7] wha,[8] kee, obay, survey, barly, vinyard, gra, (*ia*) Christyan, carrige, marrige, maneac, parlement,

[a] A collection of water. [b] An impression. [c] A joining in a garment. [d] To clip. [e] On bells. [f] In a book. [g] To work dough. [h] To run out. [i] A meadow. [k] Paltry. [l] A point. [m] Food. [n] To hearken. [o] Made of flour. [p] To uphold. [q] Large. [r] A fruit. [s] From the eye. [t] Broken. [u] A herb. [v] Did hear. [w] Did read. [x] State of the air. [y] To take food. [z] Not strong. [1] A pretence. [2] To rule. [3] Of a bridle. [4] Of them. [5] A covering. [6] To lay hold. [7] A booty. [8] From curds.

ORTHOGRAPHY. 207

(*ew*) blu,[a] bru,[b] chu, cru, deu,[c] feu,[f] fleu,[d] greu, heu,[e] kneu,[f] leud, neut, peu, screu, shreud, sleu, streu, puter, (*ie*) mischeef, peerce, preest, cavaleer, chandeleer, chavaleer, greef, theef, granadeer, di,[g] fi, li, sive, seege, releef, repreeve, retreeve, revew, vew, copyer, deaty, soldyer, beer,[h] breef, cheef, feeld, freeze,[i] frend, greeve, peer,[k] sheeld, theeve, teer,[l] weeld, pi, ti, vi, acquiesce, beleeve, greevous, feldfare, feerce, yeeld.

13. (*io*) Anxyous, dyocess, pincushon, millyon, minyon, (*oa*) oots, browd, boor,[m] boord,[n] bowt, boost, browd, clowk, cooch, cole, coorse, cowst, flowt, fole, gowt, lowd, lowf lown,[o] loth, rowd,[p] rowr, rowst, sowp, throwt, towst, bowst, hoory, ootmeal, pocher, uproor, (*oe*) Anteci, perieci, shu, canoo, do, ho, (*oi*) voyce, rejoyce, porpuse, tortise, (*oo*) brud, wul, gud, wud, fut, blud, hud, stud, dore, flore, dragune, poltrune, shalune, lusely, (*ou*) grievus, harboor, parloor, covetus, thowght, tuch, tugh, valoor, vapoor, vigoor, yung, howr, norish, truble, vigorus, armor, candor, colur, showt, abownd, cuple, groop, soop, corage, cusin, duble, florish, gowt, jurual, jurney, thogh, cort, orght, braught, poer,[q] labor, lowd, moorn, nervus, norish, toor,[r] coorse,[s] resoorce, uncooth, husewife, abownd.

14. (*ow*) Sou, so,[t] mou,[u] mo,[v] bou,[w] bo,[y] sojurn, flouers, (*tu*) congratshulate, (*ua*) asswage, perswade, gard, garantee, gardian, acqwaint, victals, (*ue*) qwench, conqwest, hu,[1] agu, gess, gest, blew[2] cu, dew,[3] flew,[4] rew, sew,[5] trew, subdew, undew, argu, tissyu, Tewsday, (*ui*) langwid, angwish, extingwish, qwite, gilt, ginea, gildhall, gide, gile, disgise, juce, frute, sute,

---

[a] Did blow. [b] To make ale. [c] A vapour. [d] Did fly. [e] To cut. [f] Did know. [g] To fall away. [h] A carriage for the dead. [i] A cornice. [k] A pillar. [l] A row. [m] A male swine. [n] A plank. [o] Anything lent. [p] A way. [q] To teem. [r] A journey. [s] Direction. [t] To cast seed into the earth. [u] A stack of corn. [v] To cut down grass. [w] An act of politeness. [y] An arch. [1] A colour. [2] Ibid. [3] Owing. [4] Of a chimney. [5] To follow.

pursute, bruse, recrute, gise, bild, bilt, gilt, purswevant, acqwit, reqwisite, biscit, circut, swete,[a] liqwid, nusance, sutor, lingwist, sangwine, acquëesce, (*uy*) obloqwe, soliloqwe, by,[b] byer, (*ay*) pla, sla, sta, stra, swa, tra, ba, ha, gra, pra, wa, ba, bra, cla, da, dra, fra, ga, ja, la, ma.

TERMINATIONS.

15. (*ce*) Accomplis, notis, justis, rise,[g] advise,[h] apprentis, avaris, lattis, malis, chalis, surplis, orifis, novis, offis, servis, verjuis, edefis, menas, solas, (*ice*) caprees, polees, justis, chalis, (*ile*) pueril,[i] volatil, ductil, facil, febril, fertil, profeel, pasteel, reptil, servil, steril, bissextil, imbecil, (*re*) sepulcher, center, luster, meter, miter, saber, specter, accouter, massacker, meager, scepter, niter, saltpeter, (*ere*) meer, seveer, (*le*) giggel, girdel, gentel, (*cle*) ankel, cirkel (*ec*) committe, debauche, (*ette*) gazet, etiquet, (*gn*) impune, maline, resine, (*igh*) invay, si, ni, ney (*ful*) shamefull, manfull, carefull, sinfull, (*ine*) macheen, mareen, magazeen, tonteen, bombazeen, rapin, marlin, engin, libertin, quaranteen, destin, doctrin, ermin, sanguin, imagin.

16. (*ive*) Festiv, passiv, plainteev, decisiv, (*ate*) agat, senat, (*ian*) guardjan, christshan, (*ir*) despare, (*ion*) connexshun, (*ence*) essens, complasens, (*ite*) hypocrit, favourit, infinit, respit, (*ure*) vultshur, vestshur, treashur, tinctshur, textshur, scriptshur, pleashur, mixtshur, meashur, leishur, lectshur, (*sia*) Russha, Prussha, Ashea, Pershea, (*tio*) rasheoshenashun, (*tion*) perfecshun, impresshun, formashun, inspirashun, institushun, modificashun, navigashun, obligashun, observashun, proporshun, nashun, meditashun, questshun,

[a] A set. [b] To purchase. [c] A foreign grain. [d] Admonitior.
Final *e* is mostly silent in English words.

digestshun, attenshun, avocatshun, demarcashun, composishun, comprehenshun, conclushun, rashional, relashun, restricshun, revelashun, revolushun, separashun, combustshun, petishun, suggestshun, transitshun, concusshun, condishun, disposishun, satisfacshun, distinctshun, tuishun, fractshun, noshun, moshun, rashonal, educashun, emoshun, estimashun, exceptshun, exhortashun, cautshun, citashun, informashun, foundashun, stashun, acshun, administrashun, admirashun, affecshun, afflicshun, alleviashun, animashun, apprehenshun, approbashun, aspirashun, expectashun, extincshun, gratificashun, habitashun, imaginashun, situashun, stashun, subjecshun, transaction, variashun, (*sion*) vacashun, successhun, penshun, decishun, divishun, compasshun, confushun, oppresshun, passhun, possesshun, pretenshun, (*cion*) suspiseun, coershun, (*vous*) rondzevoo, (*tious*) captshus, disputashus, faceshus, fictishus, flagishus, licenshus, ostentashus, propishus, sedishus, sentenshus, vexashus, infectshus, (*ous*) jealus, libellus, heinus.

17. (*cious*) Conshus, preshus, audashus, auspishus, avarishus, caprishus, silishus, contenshus, contumashus, delishus, efficashus, fallashus, feroshus, grashus, nutrishus, pernishus, rapashus, perspicashus, pertinashus, precoshus, sagashus, spashus, speshus, suspishus, tenashus, vishus, vivashus, vorashus, auspishus, meretrishus, offishus, (*ceous*) argillashus, crustashus, farinashus, fallashus, herbashus, papilionashus, saponashus, cetashus, testashus, (*tial*) marshal, speshal, parshal, essenshal, reverenshal, substanshal, (*cial*) offishal, commershal, espeshal, judishal, benefishal, (*ious*) noxshus, egregius, obnoxshus, impeus, (*cian*) logishan, magishan, musishan, optishan, physisean, politishun, (*ciate*) appresheate, assosheate, (*science*) omnishens, conshens, preshens, (*tient*) consenshent, impashent, omnishent, quoshent, (*cient*) suffishent, anshent, effishent, profishent, defishent, (*tiate*) insasheate, ingrasheate, (*seous*) nausheus, (*tuous*) spiritchus, (*sient*) transhent.

18. (*ough*) Bort, fort, sort, tho, thort, wrort, bou, clou, plow, slou, throo, do, furlo, altho, burrow,[a] thurrow, enuf, ruff,[b] sluff, tuff, coff, troff, hoc, lock,[c] shock,[d] (*eau*) buro, bewty, portmanta, bo, (*logue*) apolog, catalog, decalog, dialog, eclog, epilog, prolog, (*ogue*) voog, pedagoog, synagoog, demagoog, roog, broog, colloog, proroog, (*eague*) leeg, colleeg, teeg, (*igue*) fateeg, intreeg, (*que*) plaag, vaag, harang, tong, Haag, Praag, (*ique*) anteek, criteek, Martineek, Mosambeek, obleek, peek, uneek, (*que*) opake, grotesk, cink.

WORDS SIMILAR IN SOUND, BUT DIFFERENT IN MEANING AND SPELLING.

Join the following words to their meanings.

19. Hail, ail, ale, hale; accompt, account; accidents, accidence.
MEANINGS.— *Trouble, pain.— Strong beer.— Frozen rain.—Strong, healthy.—Regard, reckoning.—Reckoning, chances.—The rudiments of grammar.*

Axe, hacks, acts; as, has; awl, all, haul, hall.
To cut.—A tool to cut with.—Actions.—A conjunction. —Of the verb to have.—Every one—A shoemaker's tool. —A large room.—To pull.

Hare, hair, heir, ere, air, are.
What we breathe.—Before.—Of the verb am.—Of the head.—A successor to another's right.—An animal.

20. Sun, soon, son; palate, pallette, pallet.
To grind colours on.—A bed.—The organ of taste.— A male child.—The luminary of day.—Quite early.

Liar, lier, lyre; rye, wry; corps,[e] core.
One who tells lies.—One who lies down.—A musical

---

[a] A corporation. [b] Not smooth. [c] A lake. [d] A shaggy dog. [e] Pronounced core.

instrument.—Grain.—Crooked.—The inner part of fruit.—A body of soldiers.

Symbol, cymbal; night, knight.
A sign or token.—A musical instrument.—A title.—Time of darkness.

21. Sees, seas, cease, seize; is, his; two, too, to.
A preposition.—A number.—Above, also.—A pronoun.—Of the verb am.—With the eyes.—To lay hold of.—Small oceans.—To stop.

Where, were; hear, year, here, ear.
What place?—Of the verb am.—In this place.—To listen.—Twelve months.—The organ of hearing.

Hart, art, heart; write, right, wright, rite.
Just, proper.—With a pen.—A ceremony.—A man's name.—Of the verb am, skill.—The seat of life.—An animal.

22. I, eye, hoy, high; by, bye, boy, buy, buoy.
A preposition.—Lofty.—To see with.—A small vessel.—To purchase.—Near.—Presently.—To bear up, a floating mark at sea.—A lad.

Accept, except; travail, travel; toil, tile.
To receive.—To omit.—To journey.—Labour.—To cover houses with.—Fatigue.

Ewe,* hew, hue, you, yew; rains, reins, reigns.
The lower part of the back.—Governs.—Water descending from the clouds.—A tree.—A pronoun.—A colour.—To cut.—A female sheep.

23. Payer, pare, pear, peer, pair; whether, whither, wether, weather, wither.
Which.—To what place.—To fade.—A sheep.—State of the air.—Two.—To cut off.—A fruit.—One who pays.—A nobleman, an equal.

Principle, principal; dun, done; president, precedent.
A colour.—Finished.—Truth.—Chief.—An example.—One at the head of a society.

* Pronounced yö.

Whale, wail; great, grate; coarse, course.
Large.—Rough.—Progress, race-ground.—A fish.—To lament.—A fire-place.

24. Sent, scent, cent; shoe, shew; blue, blew.
One hundred.—Did send.—A smell.—For the foot.—To exhibit.—A colour.—Did blow.

Assent, ascent; there, their; ware, wear.
To agree with.—Rising.—In that place.—A pronoun.—Things for sale.—Use, worn.

Way, weigh; islands, highlands; profit, prophet.
Gain.—One who foretels.—Lands surrounded by water.—Hills.—A road.—To balance.

25. Wait, weight; apposite, opposite; seal, zeal.
Warmth.—An impression, a sea animal.—Contrary to.—Fit, proper.—To stay.—Heaviness.

Raze, raise, rays; ingenious, ingenuous; ceiling, sealing.
Of a room.—To seal.—Clever.—Generous.—To overthrow.—To lift.—Lines diverging from a centre.

Soul, sole; wreak, reek; pane, pain; cite, sight, site.
Of a shoe.—The mind.—Of a window.—Aching.—Of seeing.—To call, to quote.—Situation.—To revenge.—Steam.

26. Sore, soar, sower; threw, through; feint, faint.
Did throw.—From side to side.—A wound.—To rise.—One who sows.—A pretence.—Weary.

Wreck, rack; pale, pail; witch, which.
Destruction.—Torture.—A fence.—A bucket.—A sorceress.—A relative pronoun.

Sell, cell; mite, might; one, won; mane, main.
An insect.—Power.—To dispose of.—A cave.—A number.—Did win.—Of a horse.—Chief.

27. Seller, cellar; who, woe; Devizes, devises, devices; fain, feign, fane.

A town's name.—Desirous.—A temple.—To pretend. —He contrives.—Contrivances.—A relative pronoun.— Grief.—A room underground.—One who sells.

Practise, practice; vein, vane, vain; ire, hire, higher.

Custom, a rule in arithmetic.—To try.—Conceited.— To show which way the wind blows.—A blood vessel.— Anger.—Wages.—Loftier.

Read, reed; seen, scene; altar, alter, halter.

To peruse a book.—A large kind of grass.—Beheld. —A view.—A place for sacrifice.—To change.—A cord.

28. Naught, nought; meat, meet, mete; fore, four; boor, boar, bore.

Bad.—Nothing.—Food.—To measure.—To come together, suitable.—A number.—Before.—To make a hole. —A clown.—A male swine.

Mean, mien; beer, bier; aught, ought; plate, plait.

Manner.—Low, base, to intend.—Malt liquor.—A carriage for the dead.—Any thing.—Obligation.—A fold.—A dish, wrought gold and silver.

RULES FOR THE DIVISION OF WORDS INTO SYLLABLES.

The Rules at the head of each of the following exercises are merely for reference.

A single consonant between two vowels goes to the latter syllable; as, Pa-*per*, du-*ty*, ci-*ty*.

X is always joined to the former syllable; as, E*x*-alt, e*x*-ist.

Consonants which would be sounded at the beginning of a word, must not be separated, if the preceding vowel be long: as, nee-*dle*, de-*clare*, ta-*ble*, o-*blige*. But if the preceding vowel be short, the consonants must be separated: as, Cus-*tard*, pub-*lic*, gos-*ling*.

Two consonants, which cannot be sounded at the beginning of a word, must be separated: as, Un-der, chim-ney.

Double consonants in the middle of a word must be separated: as, Up-per, blos-som.

When several consonants come together, those which would sound at the beginning of a word, must go to the latter vowel; as, Ap-*ply*, im-*prove*, in-*struct*, trans-*gress*, parch-ment.

Two vowels, not forming a diphthong, are separated: as, Vi-al, fu-el, soci-ety.

Diphthongs must be separated from other vowels: as, Roy-al, pow-er.

Words forming compound words must be separated: as, Dew-drop, black-bird, hot-house.

Prefixes and affixes are mostly separated from the words to which they belong: as, Learn-*ed*, learn-*eth*, *be*-liev-*er*, *un*-thank-*ful*. If the separation would leave a consonant or the termination *y* standing alone, or would shorten a long vowel, this rule must not be observed. Cottages must not be divided thus, cot-tage-s, but thus, cot-ta-ges; slav-ish should be divided sla-vish; sand-y should be san-dy. Y preceded by *x* is an exception: as, Prox-y.

Ion, *tion*, *tial*, *tious*, *scious*, &c. must be divided into two syllables, though pronounced as one.

EXAMPLES OF THE LONG AND SHORT VOWELS.

Long. Pā-pĕr, bē-hāve, dū-ty. — *Short.* Cŭs-tărd, pŭb-lĭc, gŏs-lĭng.

EXERCISES.

Divide the following words into syllables.

29. Abject, ashes, bluster, cherish, concave, darken, filter, garden, helper, injure, limit, misty,

mustard, number, patron, piper, ragged, ringer, scarlet, singer, soften, stable, taper, tickle, trapping, varnish, vortex, warble, admire, compact, debase, derive, dispute, inform, protect, remark, salute, suppose, unjust, arrogant, brittleness, cocatrice, convocate, disputant, follower, gravelly, infancy, axiom, exalt, liberate, midsummer, occupy, peppermint, prevalent, regular, separate, stimulate, luxury, tunable, fixed, virtual.

30. Worshipful, yellowish, conjointly, demolish, disposal, expansive, impregnable, intrepid, hostility, reliance, respective, transgression, comprehend, introduce, action, martial, captious, mention, faction, pillion, special, ancient, patience, caution, portion, affection, essential, annually, interesting, caterpillar, aviary, momentary, condensation, opposition, continually, uncomfortable, accommodation, justification, deliberation, involuntary, universality, valetudinarian.

When there is not sufficient room at the end of a line to insert the whole of a word of more than one syllable, the word must be divided according to the above rules.

ACCENT.

By accent is meant the sounding of one syllable in a word above the rest.

The accent is marked thus ' : as, Ab'sent.

Dissyllables, or words of two syllables.

The accent is laid on the former syllable, when an affix or another word is joined to a word of one syllable: as, Child'ish, toil'some. All dissyllables ending in *y, our, ow, le, ish, e, ck, age, en, et,* accent the first. Also dissyllable nouns ending in *er,* and dissyllable words having a proper diphthong, accent the first syllable.

The accent is laid on the latter syllable, when a prefix is added to a word of one syllable: as, be-seem'. Dissyllable verbs ending in a consonant and final *e*, or in two consonants, or having a diphthong in the latter syllable, accent the last; as, es-cape', at-tend', re-veal'. Dissyllable nouns having a diphthong in the latter syllable, except a few in *ain*, accent the last.

Trissyllables, or words of three syllables.

The first syllable takes the accent when the primitive word ends in *ous, al, ion, ce, ent, ate, ude, re, le,* and *y*. Words ending in *ce, ent,* and *ate*, derived from dissylables accented on the last, accent the second syllable. The middle syllable is also accented in words ending in *ator*, and when there is a diphthong, or a vowel before two consonants, in the middle syllable.

Dissyllables formed into trissylables by adding a termination, retain the original accent.

Polysyllables, or words of more than three syllables.

Polysyllables generally follow the accent of the words from which they are derived. Those which end in *ator* mostly accent the last syllable but one. Such as end in *ion, ous, ty, ia, io,* and *cal*, accent the last syllable but two. Words ending in *le* commonly have the first syllable accented.

EXERCISES.

Divide and accent the following words.

31. Alder, grateful, actual, admittance, cyclopœdia, amber, abide, handle, advocate, alarming, punctilio, barely, abode, image, afterward, advantage, absolve, melon, animal, adventure, geographical, bedding, addict, muffle, animate, allotment, academical, blessing, address, nimble, arable,

allurement, alphabetical, boiler, open, ardent, apartment, comfortable, boldness, advice, packet, argument, appointment, amiable, bondage, afresh, passage, armoury, arrival, profitable, bony, ago, pocket, arrogate, compiler, boyish, alike, pickle, artfully, composer, bravely, alive, publish.

32. Average, confinement, broken, amass, purple, balloting, consistent, candy, arise, rambler, banishment, spectator, canker, raven, barony, creator, careful, assert, ripen, bashfulness, material, careless, attend, casement, compose, rocket, beggarly, cavern, compute, rumble, bitterness, domestic, charming, confess, rumple, blamable, annotator, childhood, confide, savage, blandishment, churlish, conform, scramble, blunderer, commentator, crumble, despoil, silken, conscious, digestion, diet, disjoint, sloven, factious, absolution, drinker, embroil, socket, casual, admiration, finger, molest, ardour, faction, application, meritorious, temperance, tolerance, utterance, violence, miscellaneous, conscious.

OF DOUBLE CONSONANTS AND FINAL E.

F, *l*, and *s*, preceded by a single vowel, are doubled when they end a word of one syllable; all other consonants remain single.

A consonant preceded by a diphthong or a long vowel is never doubled.

E, at the end of a word of one syllable, lengthens the preceding vowel, and gives the consonant a soft sound.

EXERCISES.

33. Badd, budd, cudd, dip, fib, hidd, legg, mugg, pen, rexx, sixx, tugg, dul, huf, bred, flatt, dripp, slidd, stubb, baed, caer, faem, hied, luet, mues, puer, saef, toen, tuen, vaen, vien, spil, stuf, droev, plaet,

slaev, spiet, thien, thriev, twien, bagg, cupp, dogg, figg, himm, lett, magg, tugg, ribb, sobb, tunn, hul, les, mas, dropp, plodd, slimm, thann, baed, coed, faer, hier, maec, muet, raec, saeg, toer, vael, viel, voet, fues, shril, flaek, praet, snaek, stried, thoes, throen, truec, waest.

34. Barr, burr, curr, donn, finn, lidd, napp, pinn, ridd, sodd, vann, pas, drugg, plott, slipp, thatt, baek, coek, faet, hoem, maed, naem, raeg, saem, shrimpp, sprigg, strapp, swel, thumpp, flame, price, snaer, strife, thrice, twiec, wriet, batt, butt, cut, dot, fitt, hit, lipp, pit, ripp, sapp, vatt, chinn, drumm, plugg, slit, them, bael, coel, fief, hoen, maek, mien, raek, saen, fraem, pried, spaed, striek, bedd, cagg, drabb, dabb, dug, fixx, hogg, logg, nett, hodd, robb, sott, wagg, brimm, fel, mes, chipp, flagg, plumm, slopp, then, baen, coen, fiel, hoep, maen, noed, raep, saev, shrubb, priem, pack, striev.

35. Begg, can, dadd, dunn, fogg, hopp, lopp, pott, rodd, sun, wann, cuf, wel, chop, flapp, slug, thinn, baer, coep, fien, hueg, maer, noen, raer, sied, chaf, glas, stres, priez, shaer, scoer, bett, capp, fag, fopp, hott, lott, nib, puff, cull, mil, cladd, flat, propp, slurr, bate, coer, fier, jaed, maet, noes, raez, sien, glas, pules, fluet, proeb, staeg, shoer, bidd, carr, denn, fan, fox, hugg, nipp, rott, supp, warr, fil, pil, clann, flaxx, slutt, bied, coet, foer, kiet, maez, noet, raet, sier, bles, fuem, proen, stack, sloep, bigg, catt, farr, funn, hutt, madd, nodd, hugg, rubb, tann, bul.

36. Lier, clapp, fledd, snapp, biel, cueb, laek, paeg, raer, siet, bliss, cross, glaer, proes, stael, smoet, bitt, cogg, did, fatt, gapp, jarr, man, nor, punn, rugg, tapp, waxx, mis, clip, flitt, scan, snugg, trapp, biet, cuer, fues, laem, meer, pael, raez, siez, gras, skil, strip, gloeb, pluem, staer, spoek, bobb, cott, digg, fed, map, nott, putt,

rumm, tarr, haev, tel, wil, clodd, fret, scot, spann, trimm, bred, dael, gael, laen, meet, paen, ried, soek, bogg, cann, dimm, fenn, gott, jett, man, madd, run, taxx, wedd, clogg, frogg, shagg, span, trip.

37. Boel, daem, gaem, laet, miec, paer, riep, soel, chil, stil, graec, pruen, staet, stael, boxx, cubb, dinn, few, gunn, jew, matt, nunn, ramm, sadd, ten, wen, puf, clott, from, shinn, spedd, trodd, boen, daer, gaep, lief, miel, paet, riet, soer, graep, staer, stoen, gutt, jobb, nutt, rann, sapp, tinn, wett, ful, clubb, gladd, shipp, spinn, trott, caeg, daet, gaet, liek, mien, pave, rive, suer, gros, throb, graet, scael, strange, stoer, hadd, jugg, men, padd, sat, tip, wig, kiss, muf, pul, caek, dien, gave, liem, mier, piek, roeb, take, bras, graev, scaer, scrieb, stroed.

38. Baill, aimm, baitt, brainn, hagg, jult, mett, pann, ratt, sett, topp, winn, hil, cragg, grimm, shopp, shott, whigg, caem, dier, gaez, lien, miet, piel, roed, shal, chiem, craep, graez, shaed, slied, stroev, chainn, chairr, claimm, drainn, hamm, kegg, mitt, parr, sexx, witt, giev, pus, til, cram, grainn, stabb, whimm, caen, dose, hael, loeb, dress, moed, pien, roep, taem, snuf, griep, faill, fraill, gainn, gaitt, haill, jaill, maid, maill, main, naill, paid, paill, pairr, raill, saill.

39. Kidd, mixx, patt, redd, sinn, rubb, yett, dol, tos, blott, cropp, gripp, shunn, stagg, whipp, caep, doet, paer, loer, moel, piep, roes, taep, blaed, bried, chien, craev, groep, shaem, shaek, sliem, spruec, snaill, hatt, ladd, mobb, gul, bragg, drab, gritt, shutt, starr, whitt, caer, face, paet, moep, poek, roet, tied, clas, dril, fril, shel, blaem, brien, criem, groev, smiel, taest, lapp, mopp, pegg, bel, tripp, brann, dragg, grott, skinn, stemm, whatt, caes, faed, heer, luer, poel, roev, tiel, spel, blaez, bruet, cloes, crued, shaep, smiet, trace.

40. Henn, penn, bratt, dramm, grubb, slabb, stepp, whenn, moet, troep, rued, tire, tiem, braec, change, cloeth, draek, paest, shaer, spice, traed, poer, ruel, braek, chaest, cloev, driev, braev, chied, craen, droen, place, shaev, striek, theem, plaen, slate, spier, thees.

Exceptions to the foregoing rules.—To be corrected.

Iff, eb, hass,[a] as,[b] ad, od, in,[c] yess, er, hiss,[d] butt,[e] uss, eg, of,[f] iss, bun, gass, pur, thiss, buz, thuss.

Primitive or root words of more than one syllable never end with double *l*.

In dissyllables, the consonant is doubled, when it is preceded by a short vowel, and followed by the terminations *le, y, ey, er, et,* or *on*.

Words ending in *ic, id, it, ish,* or *ity*, never double the preceding consonant.

In words beginning with *ac, af, com, ef,* or *of*, the consonant, if followed by a vowel, is always doubled.

Words beginning with *am, cat, el, ep, mod,* and *par*, never double the consonant.

V, is never doubled.

EXERCISES.

41. Aple, bannish, baner, bery, beter, bitter, buter, frollic, grovvel, pollish, bladder, bonet, buly, cammel, cary, chater, damsell, duell, finall, acsent, chery, cofer, diall, novell, slavish, comon, coper, dager, diner, folow, feny, fetter, filet, flutter, foder, ammusement, gable,[g] garet, gidy, glasy, gliter,

---

[a] Of the verb have. [b] An animal. [c] A public house. [d] A pronoun. [e] A conjunction. [f] An adverb. [g] Loud talk.

afable, gravvel, grity, moddest, guner, guter, ofering, hamer, parrable, happy, parradox, harow, poly, parragon, horid, hovvel, acording, jely, jober, jolly, acuser,

42. Kennel, ofender, ketle, ofensive, latter, lader, lavvish, ofice, leter, linet, parlour, litle, livver, maner, matter, medle, mery, midle, miler, milet, acept, mosy, muddy, mulet, mumy, netle, nipers, nevver, niple, ofer, acuse, other, parrish, peble, peper, perrish, pery, prety, piner, afair, pomel, popy, poset, poter, afirm, profer, pudle, pufer, pulet, afright, puly, pupet, quarel, quary, raddish, rally, ratle, rellish, ridle, riple, scaly, scater, scofer, scrible, scruby, seler, rivver, sevver, shagy, ellicit, triger, anoy, arive, comend, corect, efervesce, efect, opose.

Exceptions.—To be corrected.

43. Coddle, boddy, primmer, atic, accute, amoniac, frizzle, anny, propper, trafic, accumen, ammunition, trebble, coppy, choller, tyranic, accid, catle, tripple, bussy, accademy, studdy, lepper, horid, manny, considder, torid, accerbity, hury, verry, clarret, palid, affore, parot, citty, closset, flacid, affar, paricide, lilly, commet, rabit, conny, caddet, sumit, burry, plannet, commit, pitty, spinnet, skitish, honney, tennet, embellish, monney, vallet, necessity, alphabet, snapish, shaddow, rubish, winddow, petish, wagish, redish, sotish, fopish, slutish.

When words ending in silent *e* have a termination added to them, beginning with a vowel, the *e* is dropped; but if the termination begin with a consonant, the *e* is retained.

When *ous* and *able* are added to *ce* or *ge*, the silent *e* is retained,

Ee, is always retained when *ing* or *able* is added.

"Words ending in *le*, preceded by a consonant, drop *le* when *ly* is added."

When a termination is added to *y*, preceded by a consonant, the *y* is changed into *i*, except when *ing* is added. *Y* does not change when it is preceded by a vowel.

EXERCISES.

44. Add *ed* to the following words.—Age, smile, abase, abscond, absorb, adapt, advice, affront, alarm, amaze, apply, ascribe, assume, awake, collect, combine.

Join *ous*.—Pore, outrage, poison, riot, slander, advantage, miscellany, contumely, ceremony, avarice, ridicule, industry, humour, danger, spare, grace.

Join *able*.—Manage, person, ponder, profit, punish, warrant, admire. charity, misery, vary, agree, excuse, compare, remedy.

Join *ing*.—Bathe, blame, chime, graze, scrape, slice, blame, see, flee, clothe, freze, gild, go, grow, hide, make, hold.

Join *ly*.—Able, griping, gross, harmless, hasty, holy, home, honest, horrid, humble, kind, late, live, mad, melting, noble, nimble, gay.

When monysyllables, and words accented on the last syllable, end in a consonant, preceded by a single vowel, they double the consonant before another syllable beginning with a vowel. But if the additional syllable alters the accent, the consonant is not doubled.

Words ending in *l*, preceded by a single vowel, mostly double the *l*, without regard to the accent. But before *ous*, *ize*, *ist*, and *ity*, it is never doubled.

Words ending in double consonants, retain them both, except *ll* before a consonant.

Compound words are spelt the same as in their simple forms. Words, however, which end in *ll* frequently omit one *l* when compounded. *Full*, at the end of compound words, always drops one *l.*

EXERCISES.

45. Join *er, est, ish, ness, ing,* and *ful,* to the following words.—Abhor, allot, begin, admit, join, defer, forbid, inter, spell, omit, permit, recoil, refer, regret, full, mill, pull, thin, confer, infer, roll, skill, smell, chill, sweet, sour, large.

Join *ous, ize, ity.*—Brutal, formal, frugal, loyal, plural, signal, general, personal, punctual, immortal, informal, marvel.

Join the following words together.—Back-bite, dew-drop, fare-well, fire-lock, for-ward, gate-way, hence-forth, high-way, in-mate, life-less, on-set, out-cast, out-let, yard-wand, will-full, all-so, all-though, all-ready, full-fill, all-most, all-ways, chill-blain, well-fare.

EXCEPTIONS.—TO BE CORRECTED.

Wooly, woolen, wherever, christmass, martinmass, candlemass, lammass, michaelmass.

FORMATION OF THE PLURAL NUMBER OF SUBSTANTIVES.

The general rule for forming the plural number of substantives, is to add *s* to the singular: as, dove, doves.

Substantives which end in *x, o, ss,* and *ch,* when sounded soft like *sh,* form their plurals by the addition of *es*: as, fox, foxes; hero, heroes; ass, asses; church, churches.

Words ending in *io,* follow the general rule.

Substantives ending in *y,* preceded by a consonant, change the *y* into *ies*: as, beauty, beauties. But if a vowel precede the *y*, the general rule must be followed.

A few substantives change *f* and *fe* into *ves*, and some are very irregularly formed: as, man, men.

Write the plural to the following substantives.—Tax, cargo, fly, boy, calf, man, ass, echo, city, elf, woman, fish, hero, lady, delay, half, child, watch, buffalo, berry, attorney, knife, goose, leaf, potatoe, axe, volcano, life, mouse, loaf, louse, self, tooth, sheaf, foot, shelf, penny, thief, wife, wolf, umbrella, army, history, dairy, hoof, turkey, back, bard, barn, beck, band, bark, bath, belt, bend, cast, gust, mask, turn, cave, hide, lute, bench, bunch, clump, frock, length, prank, stork, cork, part, tusk, drop, corpse, dunce, frost, lodge, press, storm, waste, cord, fact, mass.

Cherub, vest, drug, seraph, plot, slip, antithesis, craft, fence, automaton, prince, shrimp, basis, sprig, trap, crisis, thump, flame, criterion, cork, farm, diæresis, hand, glance, ellipsis, chance, prong, emphasis, raft, slut, hypothesis, metamorphosis, phenomenon, appendix, arcanum, rock, axis, calx, datum, effluvium, encomium, erratum, sketch, string, genus, index, lamina, medium, curl, spar, bush, magus, memorandum, text, match, trench, blush, chink, crutch, flitch, ridge, branch, dance, notch, ditch, radius, stamen, bush, dash, church, stratum, vortex, die (*for play*), die (*for coining*), watch, wish, hatch, pinch, stitch, sash, dish, snatch, hitch, brush, envoy, gravy, influx, jury, kinsman, navy, Mr., beau, virtuoso.

FORMATION OF THE FEMININE GENDER OF SUBSTANTIVES.

The feminine gender is mostly formed by changing the masculine termination into *ess:* as, abbot, abbess.

Sometimes the sex is shown by a different word: as, bachelor, maid.

Some substantives change *or* into *rix:* as, executor,

executrix. And some by adding another substantive to the masculine and the feminine: as, a cock-sparrow, a hen-sparrow. Sometimes the sex is denoted by joining *he* to the substantive for the masculine, and *she* for the feminine: as, a he-goat, a she-goat.

Form the feminine gender of the following masculine substantives.—Bachelor, husband, abbot, landgrave, a cock-sparrow, boar, king, actor, lion, a man servant, boy, lad, administrator, marquis, a he-goat, brother, lord, adulterer, master, a he-bear, ambassador, a male-child, arbiter, mayor, patron, male-descendants, baron, peer, bridegroom, poet, benefactor, priest, caterer, prince, chanter, prior, conductor, prophet, buck, man, count, protector, bull, deacon, shepherd, bullock, steer, milter, songster, duke, cock, nephew, ram, elector, sorcerer, dog, singer, emperor, sultan, drake, enchanter, earl, sloven, executor, tiger, father, governor, traitor, friar, stag, heir, tutor, gander, uncle, hero, hart, viscount, wizard, hunter, votary, host, widower, horse, Jew.

FINIS.

 www.ingramcontent.com/pod-product-compliance
Lightning Source LLC
Chambersburg PA
CBHW080436110426
42743CB00016B/3178